HELP! MY COMPUTER IS BROKEN

HELP! MY COMPUTER IS BROKEN

BARRY COLLINS

First published in 2020 by
Raspberry Pi Trading Ltd,
Maurice Wilkes Building,
St. John's Innovation Park,
Cowley Road,
Cambridge, CB4 0DS

Publishing Director: Russell Barnes • Editors: Phil King, Simon Brew • Sub Editor: Nicola King
Design: Critical Media • Illustrations: Sam Alder with Brian O Halloran
CEO: Eben Upton

ISBN: 978-1-912047-90-1

CONTENTS

ABOUT THE AUTHOR

Barry Collins has been a technology journalist for more than 20 years.

He's written for most of the UK's leading tech publications, including PC Pro, ComputerActive, Which?, Web User, and many more. He's a former editor of PC Pro and was assistant editor of The Sunday Times' technology section. He's now the co-editor of The Big Tech Question, a site designed to answer people's tech queries – in a similar vein to this book.

Barry makes regular appearances as a tech pundit on TV and radio, including on Newsnight, BBC Radio 5 Live, The Chris Evans Show, and many more.

He lives in Sussex with his partner, two daughters, a greyhound, and a cupboard full of computing kit that he refuses to throw away because it will definitely come in handy one day.

ABOUT THIS BOOK

Let's get the apology out of the way first: we're sorry. Sorry because from the mere act of picking up this book and flicking through it in the bookstore, or scanning its first few pages on Amazon, we can tell that you've been there.

You've suffered from one of those knotty computer problems that make you want to shove your fist through the screen, just so you never have to see that impenetrable error message ever again. We feel your pain. How many sugars do you want in your tea?

We can't promise to solve all of your computing ills – there's not enough ink and paper left in the world to cover every conceivable computer fault. But we can promise that we've covered most of the major problems that might befall a PC or laptop and have provided no-nonsense advice on how to deal with them.

What's more, we deal with those problems without burying you under an avalanche of jargon. You won't need a master's in computer science to work through our solutions. You won't need a teenager on speed dial to explain what a SCSI port is. You won't even need to know that SCSI is pronounced 'scuzzy', like the state of said teenager's bedroom.

Instead, we'll explain everything in (to use that hackneyed phrase) plain English. And on each answer, you'll find a brief 'What can I do about it?' set of bullet points, that give you an overview of the potential solutions before you dive into the full explanation.

As we said before, we don't have all the answers – but we'll give you advice on where to find them if you come across a problem that's not covered in these pages. And without wishing to sound like doom-mongers, chances are you will come across one or more of the problems covered in this book during your computing lifetime. So, if you're still thumbing through in the bookstore, why not take this book home now and be prepared for the day when the difficulty strikes?

We'll pop the kettle on, just in case.

WHY IS MY LAPTOP NOT TURNING ON?

Let's start at square one. After all, if the computer isn't even firing up, the rest of the problems we solve in this book are pretty academic.

Here, we're talking about a computer that shows no signs of life when you press the power button – the screen's not lighting up, there are no funny beeps, it's showing fewer vital signs than a bar of soap.

First, check the power cable is fully inserted into the power port, and that any cable connections in the power brick are firmly in place. Even a slightly dislodged cable may not provide a charge.

Many modern laptops charge via a USB-C port, but you need to ensure that the power supply is adequate. The charger that comes with your mobile phone, for instance, may not be sufficient to charge the laptop. Be sure to use the charger that came with your laptop, not any old USB charger you can lay your hands on.

It's also possible that not every USB-C port on your laptop accepts the charge. Try moving the power cable to a different port if one isn't bringing the machine back to life.

If the laptop hasn't been used for a few weeks or months, it may need a while plugged into the charger before it will come back to life. Chromebooks are particularly prone to this type of sulk. The Google Pixelbook often needs to be plugged in for several hours before it will resume normal operation if it's been left dormant for a fortnight or so, which can be enormously frustrating.

On laptops with removable batteries, check the battery is firmly locked in place. Most will have sliders that can be easily dislodged in a bag, breaking the connection between battery and laptop.

One final thing to try on laptops with removable batteries is draining any residual electricity. Unclip the battery (if possible), remove the power cable, and then hold down the power button for 30 seconds or so, to make sure any residual energy in the laptop is sapped. Now plug the power cable back in, but don't put the battery back in. Fire up the laptop and – if all is well – shut it down again. Now put the battery back and power her up once more.

If none of the above breathe life back into your laptop, a hardware failure of some sort is likely. It could be the charger, the battery, or something more fundamentally afoot inside the laptop itself. Brace yourself for a visit to the repair shop, but bear in mind that many of today's sealed-unit laptops aren't easy for even the professionals to fix.

What can I do about it?
- Check power cables are plugged in securely
- Only use the supplied charger
- Leave the battery to charge for a few hours
- Drain residual electricity from the computer

WHY IS MY DESKTOP COMPUTER NOT TURNING ON?

Unlike laptops, desktop computers don't have batteries that can run down, so a complete failure to even turn on is not a great sign.

We're talking about a PC exhibiting no signs of life – if you're seeing something on screen, hearing weird beeps, or you're getting bewildering error messages, we'll deal with those later. Right now, we're focusing on a computer that's to all intents and purposes dead.

First thing to check is that all the power cords are plugged in securely. Desktop PCs will often have a kettle-plug type socket that fits into the back of the computer – just make sure that hasn't come even slightly dislodged, as that can prevent a PC from starting.

Also try unplugging peripherals such as printers, scanners, USB hubs, or any other device other than keyboard, mouse, and screen. An electrical fault with one device can prevent a PC from booting.

If that fails to bring it to life, then there may be a problem with the computer's power supply. If the PC case has been banged or knocked, it's possible the cable(s) connecting the power supply to the computer's motherboard has come loose.

If you feel comfortable opening up your PC and having a poke around, you're normally looking for white plastic connectors that have popped off the motherboard (the main circuit board). Every power supply is different, but search YouTube for 'replacing a PC power supply' and you'll find videos that show you how they plug in. If you're not confident, take it to a repair shop – it should be a cheap fix if it's just a loose cable.

Power supplies themselves can fail, and this is normally a job for the repair shop unless you're very confident you know what you're doing. If you're planning to replace the supply yourself, just beware that all power supplies are not born equal – you'll need to match the wattage of the supply you're replacing. It's very much at your own risk.

Other internal devices such as memory modules or graphics cards becoming unseated can prevent a computer from firing up. A gentle push on the components might be enough to put them back in place, but take care. The connectors are fragile and pushing too hard can be an expensive mistake.

What can I do about it?
- Check all cables are securely connected
- Unplug everything except screen, mouse, and keyboard
- Open the PC and check power supply connectors

WHY IS MY LAPTOP'S KEYBOARD NOT WORKING?

Seen any guilty-looking toddlers lurking suspiciously close to your laptop with once-full glasses of juice? Accidental spills are one of many reasons why your laptop's keyboard can turn into little more than a jumbled alphabet, but the fault isn't always as obvious as a MacBook drowning in Ribena.

The first thing to determine is whether a keyboard fault has knocked out the entire keyboard or only certain keys. If it's a cluster of keys alone, it's very likely something has been spilled on the keyboard. Turn the laptop off and remove the battery (if possible), lay the keyboard upside down on a cloth or kitchen paper, and let the system dry thoroughly for 48 hours. Use a dry brush around the affected area to remove any debris. With any luck, the keyboard will return to full health when dry. If it doesn't, a trip to the repair shop beckons.

If the entire keyboard is kaput, it's likely something else is afoot. Keyboards are normally connected to the computer's motherboard by a thin ribbon-like interface, and it's not unheard of for these to pop off – especially if the laptop has been dropped or banged.

Not so long ago, you could normally remove a few screws on the base of the laptop, wear a static strip, and put the ribbon back in place yourself. These days laptops are generally sealed units that require special tools to prise apart. A trip to the repair shop is likely to be necessary.

Before you load the laptop in the car and drive to your local geek emporium, there is something else you should try to rectify a whole keyboard failure on Windows laptops. Turn the laptop off, power it back on again, and then quickly press the key on your laptop that enters the computer's BIOS (or setup) menu – the key differs from manufacturer to manufacturer, but **F2**, **F10**, and **DEL** are commonly used.

If the laptop will enter the BIOS menu, then the fault is likely with the keyboard's software driver, not the keyboard itself. Leave the BIOS setup menu and boot back into Windows as normal. Plug in an external USB keyboard (borrow one if you don't have one lying around) and open the Device Manager by typing that phrase into the Windows search menu and selecting the relevant option.

In the Device manager, look for keyboards, find your laptop's main keyboard (normally called Standard PS/2 keyboard), and right-click on it. Select 'Uninstall device'. Restart the computer and Windows should – fingers crossed – automatically reinstall the keyboard. If not, right-click on keyboards in the Device Manager again and select Scan For Hardware Changes. That should reinstall the keyboard driver and hopefully resolve your problem.

What can I do about it?
- Switch the laptop off and dry any spills
- Reinstall the keyboard's software driver

WHAT ARE THOSE BLACK DOTS ON MY SCREEN?

Fetch a black armband, prepare a heartfelt speech, dig out those Celine Dion CDs: we're sorry to tell you that one or more of your screen's pixels has passed away.

Today's computer displays are made up of millions of tiny dots, called pixels. If one of those pixels fails or gets stuck (we'll come to that in a minute), you'll either see a tiny, permanent black dot on your screen or one that's stuck on a particular colour.

They're easier to spot when your screen is displaying a single colour. Visit **color.aurlien.net** in your web browser and press **F11** (in Windows only) to make the browser window full-screen and the display will flip through various single colours, helping you to identify if a pixel has passed away or needs life support.

There's not much you can do to rescue a completely dead pixel. Most screen and laptop manufacturers will have a dead pixel policy in their warranty that allows you to replace the device if a certain number of pixels fail. That's why it's important to test new screens and laptops when you first buy them, before the warranty expires or your right to return faulty products lapses.

Stuck pixels that are locked to a particular colour can be rescued, however. There are various utilities that blast the screen with lots of different colours to unjam stubborn pixels. One of the simplest to use is **jscreenfix.com** – you simply drag the square over the stuck pixel area and leave the utility to work its magic for ten minutes. With any luck, you'll have a fully restored pixel by the time you've made a brew.

Even if you're lumbered with a dead or stuck pixel, it's generally not the end of the world these days. Screens are now so high-resolution that even one or two faulty pixels are barely noticeable. But like that mark on a freshly painted wall, once you've seen them, you can't stop looking at them...

What can I do about it?

- Visit **color.aurlien.net** to check for dead or stuck pixels
- Go to **jscreenfix.com** to unjam stuck pixels

WHY IS MY COMPUTER MAKING STRANGE BEEPS WHEN I SWITCH IT ON?

Does your computer sound like a supermarket checkout till every time you turn it on?

That beeping noise is the power-on self-test (POST) that every computer performs when it's first switched on. It's a mini-MOT the computer conducts by itself to check everything is working properly before it launches into Windows. It happens so quickly you won't even notice it when everything is fine, but when something is amiss, you'll hear a series of beeps and may also see an on-screen warning.

The number of beeps you hear is indicative of the problem. But here's the thing: every different computer manufacturer has a different set of beep codes. Even different models made by the same manufacturer can have different codes.

For example, at the time of writing, two beeps on a Dell Inspiron laptop indicates no memory (RAM) detected, three beeps is a motherboard chipset failure, and four beeps signals a memory failure. On a Lenovo IdeaPad laptop, however, a basic memory failure is indicated by one short beep, followed by three short beeps, followed by another two beeps!

If we tried to list every beep code for every manufacturer, this book would be the size of an encyclopaedia. Instead, our best advice if you hear strange beep codes when you fire up your computer is to note down the pattern, then do a Google search for your laptop manufacturer and model name, followed by beep codes (i.e. 'Lenovo ThinkPad beep codes').

What can I do about it?
● Make a note of the beep pattern (e.g. three short beeps)
● Google your computer manufacturer and model name, then 'beep codes'

HOW CAN I TELL IF MY COMPUTER IS OVERHEATING?

There are telltale signs that a computer is getting too hot – and it's not sweat pouring out of the USB ports.

The first sign is instability and sudden shutdowns. Today's computers are loaded with built-in thermometers and are programmed to shut themselves down if a core component becomes too toasty, thus preventing the whole system turning into a smoke machine.

Other signs are funny smells emanating from the vents or the fans constantly running at full pelt. Don't be paranoid – most laptops or PCs will fire up their fans if you're doing something heavy-duty, such as playing 3D games or editing video, or if it's been running for a long while. But if the fans are screaming from the moment you turn the thing on, or after it's been left idle for a while, you might have a problem.

Free utilities let you check the temperature of your computer's processor (CPU) and graphics card (if you've got one) – the two chief suspects in an overheating system. The free Speccy (**ccleaner.com/speccy**) is one such utility for Windows systems.

Once Speccy is installed, click on the CPU section on the left-hand side of the window and look for the temperatures. If your CPU temperature is constantly displayed in red figures (90°C or above), something is up. Switch it off to prevent further damage and get it checked.

What can I do about it?
- Download Speccy
- Check CPU and graphics card temperatures
- Switch off if too hot

WHY IS MY LAPTOP'S TOUCHPAD NOT WORKING?

Like a parent trying to wipe chocolate off a child's face with a tissue, you're swiping at your laptop's touchpad and nothing's happening. That pointy arrow on the screen isn't moving a jot. Let's try to work out what's gone wrong.

First, it's possible that you've accidentally deactivated the touchpad (sometimes referred to as a trackpad). Some laptops have a little switch that turns off the touchpad; others have strange key combos that disable the device – a feature designed for those who prefer to work with a mouse or trackpoint and want to make sure that accidental presses on the touchpad don't send the cursor zinging across the screen.

To check if you've accidentally knocked out the touchpad, type 'mouse' in the Windows 10 search box and open the mouse settings (you might need to plug in an external mouse to navigate the screens if you don't have a touchscreen). Click on Additional Mouse Options in the top-right corner and look for options to enable/disable the touchpad.

On Apple laptops, you'll find the trackpad options by clicking on the Apple icon in the top-left corner of the screen, selecting System Preferences, and choosing Trackpad.

If Windows is reporting the touchpad is enabled, it's time to check the touchpad's software drivers. Windows updates often knock out the touchscreen or touchpad on Lenovo devices, for example, until you run an update on the laptop that installs all new drivers.

Most laptop manufacturers will have their own utility that checks for driver updates. Lenovo's is called Lenovo Vantage, for instance; Dell's is simply called Dell Update. Run that application and install any available updates for the touchpad or pointing devices.

Our old friend the Windows Device Manager can also reveal touchpad troubles. Open the Device Manager by searching for it, click on Mice and Pointing Devices, and look for the touchpad (it might be called Synaptics Pointing Device or something similar). Right-click and select Update Driver if it's reporting a problem.

Finally, it's worth removing all external mice – including Bluetooth mice – to see if that solves your problem. It's daft, but some laptops knock out the touchpad in favour of an external mouse.

If none of the above work, it's possible there's a hardware failure. Brace yourself for an expensive trip to the repair shop or get used to using an external mouse.

What can I do about it?

- Check the mouse settings to make sure the touchpad hasn't been accidentally deactivated
- Update the touchpad's drivers
- Remove external mice

WHY IS THERE NO SOUND COMING FROM MY LAPTOP'S BUILT-IN SPEAKERS?

Hello silence, my old friend… If your laptop is intent on playing the sound of silence even when you're trying to blast out AC/DC, it's time to start fiddling with your sound settings.

First, let's work through the obvious, just to be sure you've not done something silly. Make sure any headphones or speakers plugged into the laptop are removed or switched off. Bluetooth headphones and speakers can catch you out here, as there's obviously no lead sprouting from the laptop.

Most laptop keyboards will have a mute button that it's easy to accidentally activate, especially as some of them are on the row of function buttons directly above the numbers. Look for a little speaker icon with a line through it and push the button to see if that restores the speakers.

You can also use the Windows settings to check if your speakers are silenced. In the row of tiny icons next to the clock, look for the speaker icon and click on it. Drag the volume slider up if it's down on the left-hand side. On Macs, the speaker icon is found in the menu bar at the top of the screen.

If the volume appears to be turned up, but you still can't hear any sound from the video/music you're trying to play, it's time to dig a little deeper. If you're playing the media in a web browser, it's possible the browser tab is muted. Today's web browsers have tools designed to silence those furiously irritating ads that play in the background, but these can sometimes result in content you want to hear being accidentally blocked.

In browsers such as Chrome or Firefox, a little speaker icon will appear at the top of the tab if content is playing, or a speaker with a line through it will be shown if it's been muted. In Chrome, you can right-click on that tab's header and select Unmute Site to restore volume; in Firefox you merely have to click on that tiny speaker icon in the tab header.

Likewise, if you're using an app such as Spotify or iTunes to play music, just check there are no mute buttons activated from within the app itself. These can be tricky to spot. Spotify will mute if you click the speaker icon next to the volume slider, which is easy to do by accident.

If all else fails, Windows 10 users can run a troubleshooter to see if the operating system can repair the audio. Type 'troubleshooter' into the search bar and click on Troubleshoot Settings. Now click Additional Troubleshooters and select Playing Audio and Windows will have a stab at sorting out any problems.

What can I do about it?
- Switch off any Bluetooth headphones or speakers nearby
- Check the computer's volume settings
- Check browser tabs or applications aren't muted
- Run the Windows troubleshooter

WHY IS THERE NO SOUND COMING FROM MY COMPUTER'S EXTERNAL SPEAKERS?

Most laptop speakers would be drowned out by a squirrel nibbling an acorn in the back garden, which is why many folks will connect a pair of thumping external speakers to their computer. But what if they're not working?

First, we'd urge you to read the previous question, which ticks off many of the problems that you might encounter with getting sound to play on either built-in or external speakers.

Let's deal first with wired speakers, ones that are plugged into either the headphone jack or via USB. We're going to start with a lemon-sucker, but you have checked they're plugged in, right? Some wired speakers don't need external power, many do. Just make sure the power's switched on or the power cable hasn't leapt out of the back of them.

Next, we need to make sure your computer's got the right set of speakers selected. A common problem on Windows computers is that the PC's trying to send sound out through the monitor's speakers... even if the monitor doesn't have speakers. In Windows 10, click on the little speaker icon near the clock, click the up arrow next to the name of the speaker at the top, and just make sure your external speakers are the ones currently selected.

On a Mac, click on the Apple icon, choose System Preferences, click on the Sound icon, select the Output tab, and choose the speakers that you wish to disturb the neighbours with.

If it's Bluetooth speakers that are giving you problems, then you need to check the computer's still talking to them. Type 'Bluetooth' into the Windows search bar, open the Bluetooth settings and check that your chosen speakers are listed as connected under the Audio section. If they've gone walkabout, first check the speakers are actually turned on – many will switch themselves off after a short period of inactivity. If they're on, click the 'Add Bluetooth or other device' button at the top of the screen and see if you can get them to reconnect.

Bluetooth devices can be painfully stubborn. If your computer can't detect them, it's worth rebooting both the speakers and computer and trying again. Also check if your speakers have a specific pairing routine that you need to enable for the computer to see them in the first place – a quick search online should help.

What can I do about it?
- Check power to the speakers
- Ensure the right speakers are selected in Windows/macOS
- Check the Bluetooth connection for wireless speakers

WHY IS MY MOUSE NOT WORKING?

If you're a desktop computer user, you're pretty stuck if your mouse suddenly decides to go on strike. Here's how to get yourself out of a mouse hole.

First, assuming you've got a laser mouse that's plugged into the computer, flip the rodent over and check if the lights are on.

If there's no sign of life, it suggests the mouse isn't getting power from the computer. Try plugging the mouse into a different USB port.

If you're plugging the mouse into a USB hub, trying connecting it directly to a port on the computer instead.

If you're using a wireless mouse, again flip it over and look for the vital signs (chest compressions and mouth-to-mouth are unnecessary). Obviously, you need to make sure the batteries are topped up – today's mice last so long between charges/battery replacements that it's easy to forget the things don't run on pure magic.

If your mouse has a little Bluetooth receiver that you plug into the computer, again try moving that to a different USB port.

If a wireless mouse appears to be alive and well, but it's not doing mousey things, then it's time to check the wireless connection. On Windows, type 'Bluetooth' into the search bar, select the Bluetooth settings, and see if your mouse is listed in the menu. If not, try adding the device afresh.

Now, at this point, you might be thinking, 'Hang on, pal. If my mouse isn't working, how am I meant to open search and navigate menus?' Well, Windows has a feature that allows you to use your keyboard's cursor arrow keys to move the mouse. Hold down the **ALT**, **LEFT SHIFT**, and **NUM LOCK** keys simultaneously and it should give you the option to turn on Mouse Keys. Press the **SPACE** bar or the **ENTER** key to confirm that you do wish to turn them on.

If the Bluetooth connection appears to be fine, it's worth kicking the tyres of our old friend the software drivers. Search for Device Manager, open the Mouse and Pointing Devices section and look for any exclamation marks against your mouse, which is always a bad sign. Click on the mouse and try updating drivers, or uninstalling the device and restarting again.

What can I do about it?

- Try different USB ports
- Make sure the batteries are charged
- Use Windows' Mouse Keys to help you diagnose faults

WHY ARE GAMES RUNNING REALLY SLOWLY ON MY COMPUTER?

Fortnite taking a fortnight to load? FIFA matches not even making it to kick-off? Running games on a Windows PC or Mac is not as simple as many people think.

While almost any computer you can lay your hands on will happily play a few hands of Solitaire or smash your self-confidence at chess, only high-powered PCs will play the latest 3D games. Computers aren't like consoles: not every game you can buy for them will play on every machine.

The determining factor is normally the computer's graphics chip. Laptops, by and large, don't have dedicated graphics cards – they use what is known as integrated graphics – which means they're usually not up to playing the latest 3D games at playable frame rates (how many times per second the screen is refreshed to make the action appear smooth).

If you want to play 3D action games such as Fortnite or Call of Duty on a laptop, you need to look for one with dedicated graphics – companies such as Dell's Alienware or Asus will happily sell you one of these, but you'll do very well to get any change out of a thousand pounds.

Can you add graphics capability to a laptop with integrated graphics? Not easily. There are a few external graphics card (eGPU) units out there from companies such as Razer and Blackmagic, but they're expensive, rely on ports that many cheap laptops won't have, and you'll need a relatively nippy laptop to take full advantage of them in the first place. It's not something we'd generally recommend.

Desktop tower computer are more suited to gaming as they can be fitted with dedicated graphics cards and they don't always cost the Earth. A decent budget graphics card can be had for around £100–£150, although it's important to check that your computer has the right slot to accommodate a graphics card.

What if you've got a computer with a decent graphics card but games are still struggling? There are a few things you can do to make them more playable. Dive into the game's own settings menu and dial down the graphics quality – you might sacrifice mist sweeping across landscapes or other special effects, but at least the game will be playable. If that doesn't work, try reducing the resolution – with fewer 'pixels' for the graphics card to push around, the game should run more smoothly.

If you want to play the latest PC games on any computer, no matter how old or underpowered, check out a streaming service such as Shadow (**shadow.tech**) or Google Stadia (**store.google.com/stadia**). These run the games in massive data centres and then stream them to your computer, much like a Netflix video. You'll need a decent fibre broadband connection to take advantage of them, though.

What can I do about it?
- Invest in a new graphics card (if possible)
- Dial down the game's graphics quality or resolution
- Consider a games-streaming service

CAN I MAKE MY LAPTOP FASTER BY UPGRADING ITS MEMORY?

A few years back, the answer to this question would have been an almost certain yes. Most laptops would have a little compartment on the base that you could unscrew and pop in a couple of new memory chips to give your laptop more zip. Now, it's not so clear cut.

The problem is that most laptop designs these days are sealed units. Memory compartments are now the exception rather than the rule. That means that opening up a laptop is often now a job for the professionals.

What's more, even if a repair shop could prise apart your laptop, there's no guarantee even they would be able to upgrade the memory. The RAM is often soldered or glued to the motherboard, making it impossible to swap out chips. On many laptop designs, you're pretty much stuck with what you've got.

That's not to say it's not worth trying. Crucial's System Scanner tool will tell you in a heartbeat if your computer's memory can be upgraded or not. You'll find it at: **uk.crucial.com/gbr/en/systemscanner**.

If you do have an accessible memory slot, make sure you load the computer with the right type of memory. Not only does it need to be the right type (DDR3, DDR4 etc), it needs to be the right speed. You can't just slam any old memory chips you find on eBay in there. Again, Crucial's tool will tell you precisely what you need inside your system.

You'll probably need to double the complement of memory inside in your laptop to see any notable difference. At the time of publication in 2020, 8GB is the minimum amount of memory we'd recommend for a Windows or Mac laptop. 16GB should be plenty for most day-to-day computing jobs, with 32GB or more reserved for those who are doing real heavy lifting, such as intensive graphics work or video editing.

By the way, you may remember a Windows feature called ReadyBoost, where you could plug in a compatible USB memory stick and have it act like extra memory. That is still available, although in

our tests its benefits were next to negligible. Google ReadyBoost if
you want to give it a crack.

What can I do about it?

- Try Crucial's system scanner to see if you can upgrade
  your memory
- Make sure you buy the right type
- Double the quantity you already have to see a noticeable boost

WHY WON'T THE USB PORT ON MY COMPUTER CHARGE MY PHONE?

The only thing that never seems to get better about smartphones is their battery life. Today's phones are like milkmen: they're shattered by lunchtime, which means you'll often need to plug the phone in for a quick charge at your desk. But why is the phone not charging – or charging very slowly – when you plug it into your PC or laptop?

This basically boils down to power. Although the USB port on your computer looks the same as the one on your phone charger, the current output is very different.

Some older USB ports on computers may deliver little or no power. Some companies disable USB ports on their computers because they don't want staff plugging in disk drives and taking home sensitive information. And even fully functioning USB ports may not have enough juice to top up your phone as quickly as you're used to.

Many of today's posher phones – and even more economical ones – use a system called Fast Charge that blasts the battery from empty to half-charged in as little as ten or 20 minutes. But, for that, you need the charger the phone is supplied with; you won't get that kind of performance by plugging your phone into a computer's USB port.

If your phone isn't charging at all from a computer's USB port, and you're sure the port is working, then there are a few things to check. First, the computer normally has to be powered on (we'll come back to this in a sec). Computers that have put themselves to sleep will often cut power to USB ports, which might explain why you left your phone on charge while you went to lunch and it's only added 2% by the time you got back to your desk.

You can fiddle with your computer's power management settings (search for 'power' in the Windows 10 Start menu to access the relevant settings), although you might reflect that there are more environmentally friendly ways to charge a phone than keeping a desktop computer running.

Some laptops do allow you to charge your phone from the laptop's battery, even when the lid of the device is shut and the computer's on standby. Look for a little symbol with a lightning squiggle inside a battery next to the port, which indicates that it can be used for such purposes. Obviously, your laptop battery will need to have sufficient charge if it's not connected to the mains supply.

This so-called Always-on USB feature sometimes needs to be switched on in your computer's settings. The utilities that computer manufacturers supply with their systems (such as Lenovo's Vantage) will normally have an option to turn this feature on or off.

What can I do about it?
- Don't let the computer lapse into sleep/standby mode
- Check you're using the correct USB port
- Make sure Always-on USB is enabled

WHY WON'T MY COMPUTER CONNECT TO THE WI-FI?

Wi-Fi sometimes makes you weep for the days when the only way to get the internet was to lash your laptop to the phone socket.

This question could almost be a book in itself, because there are so many potential answers. And even when people sometimes think their 'Wi-Fi is broken', it's not the Wi-Fi at all, but the internet connection to the router itself. But let's try and work through this knotty one together and see if we can get things back to normal.

First, we need to ensure that the Wi-Fi router is working properly in the first place. Can other devices in the home (smartphones, tablets) get a Wi-Fi connection? If all or only some of your devices cannot connect, it's a router problem. Try restarting the router (yes, switching it off and on again) as routers can be temperamental beasts.

Assuming it's only your computer that's not getting a Wi-Fi signal, then we need to look for reasons why. Some laptops have a Wi-Fi switch that turn off the Wi-Fi radios, which you might have accidentally flicked. Look for a little slider, often on the side or front of a laptop, with a little Wi-Fi symbol next to it.

Other laptops allow you to kill the Wi-Fi radio with a key combo or function key. On a Lenovo ThinkPad, for example, the **F8** key will knock out the wireless radios, which is easy to mistakenly press when you're shooting for a number on the top row of the keyboard. Again, look for buttons with Wi-Fi symbols that might help you get back in the game.

Windows and Macs both have menus that allow you to see the available Wi-Fi networks, in case your computer has simply dropped off the network for whatever reason. In Windows 10, look for a little Wi-Fi symbol in the tray next to the clock in the bottom-right of the screen. If you click on that, you should see your Wi-Fi network and be able to click on it to reconnect. On Macs, look for the little Wi-Fi symbol at the top of the screen. If your network isn't appearing and you know you're within Wi-Fi range, restarting the computer can often solve the problem.

If you can't see any Wi-Fi networks at all on your computer, there might be a problem with the wireless card. The first thing to do is to check for any recent updates to the software drivers for your wireless card. In Windows 10, type 'updates' into the search menu next to the Start button, choose Check for Updates, and then View Update History. Under Driver Updates, see if any updates to wireless cards have been applied recently that could be the source of a problem.

If there have been, search for Device Manager, click on Network Adapters and look for your wireless card – it will be called something like Intel Dual Band Wireless. Right-click on that, select Properties, click on the Driver tab, and select Roll Back Driver. This should (fingers crossed, say three Hail Marys) return the driver to its previous state and – after a system restart – put you back online.

It's not unknown for Windows updates to cause problems as serious as knocking out Wi-Fi cards in computers, either. Windows 10

Update 1903, released in the summer of 2019, disabled a number of wireless cards, forcing owners to rewind the Windows update to get their computer back online.

What can I do about it?

- Check you've not accidentally disabled Wi-Fi
- Restart both router and computer
- Wind back any recent wireless card driver updates

MY PC IS ASKING ME TO UPDATE THE BIOS – SHOULD I DO IT?

Firstly, well done. You're right to be suspicious of any impromptu pop-up window on your PC asking you to install anything. Many a good PC has been ruined by a click in haste.

So who's this BIOS fella, we hear you ask, and why does he need updating?

BIOS stands for Basic Input/Output System. It's basically the software that the computer runs from the very moment you press the power button, even before Windows gets involved.

If you've ever had to do some serious troubleshooting with your PC, you may well have been asked to fire up the BIOS screen, which is normally done by pressing one of the **F** function keys before Windows loads. In there, you'll find advanced options, such as choosing which operating system to load first (if you have more than one installed), which disk to boot from, and options to recover a corrupted Windows installation.

If you're lucky, you'll never have to get your hands dirty with the BIOS screen. Like tax returns, life is generally much easier without it. However, from time to time, your computer may automatically download an update for its BIOS and it's a good idea to install these.

Before you click OK, a little health warning. Just make 100% sure this isn't a fake pop-up that's been generated by an iffy website you're browsing. Antivirus software is pretty good at rooting out this stuff, but the odd one can slip through the net and it could leave you with some nasty ransomware or other hideous mess to deal with. If you're not absolutely sure, click No or Cancel and see if the same pop-up comes back later, when you're not browsing the web. That's normally a good sign it's genuine.

It's paramount that the BIOS update is installed cleanly and isn't interrupted – if your BIOS is corrupted, Windows won't boot and you face a world of pain getting your PC back in working order. Therefore, if you're running a laptop on battery power, plug it in before you click OK just to make sure the battery doesn't run dry during the process. Make sure you've saved any work and shut all your programs down, too.

The BIOS update should only take a minute or two and you might see code flashing across a black screen while the update is in progress. The PC will need to restart itself at the end of the update. You can go away and make a cup of tea while all this is going on – it's statistically proven* that a watched update is 87% more likely to go wrong.

(*Proven may be stretching it.)

What can I do about it?
- Make sure it's not a fake pop-up
- Save all work and close all programs
- Plug a laptop in and then run the update

HOW DO I IMPROVE THE BATTERY LIFE OF MY LAPTOP?

If your laptop battery is not exactly an Energiser Bunny, but lasts about as long as a rabbit in the headlights, there are things you can do to extend the period before it runs out of puff.

We'll deal with replacing your laptop battery in the next question. Suffice it to say that if the battery has been in the laptop for years, has had heavy use and now peters out in a matter of minutes, much of what we discuss below is probably not going to make a solid difference. All batteries have a finite life and it might be time for a replacement.

However, if you've got a relatively spritely set of cells, then the following tips should help eke out the maximum battery life:

Dim the screen

The screen is one of the biggest battery burners on your laptop. Windows and Mac laptops normally dim the screen automatically when on battery power, but you can take manual control and dim it further. If you're in a dark train carriage, for example, you probably won't need much more than minimum brightness to see your laptop screen clearly. Look for a key marked with what looks like a sun and a minus sign to turn the brightness down. Failing that, type 'display' into Windows search and use the slider to adjust brightness.

Switch off Wi-Fi and Bluetooth

Although the wireless radios on modern laptops are much less battery-intensive than those of yesteryear, they will still trickle power away. If you're working on a train or in a café without Wi-Fi or wireless gadgets, then switching those radios off will keep more battery power in the bank.

Some laptops have a physical switch that lets you turn Wi-Fi off, others have a keyboard combo. However, the easiest way to switch both off in Windows 10 is to put the laptop in Flight Mode. Click on the little speech bubble in the bottom right-hand corner of the screen and click the Flight Mode button that appears, to disable Wi-Fi and Bluetooth.

Macs are seemingly air sick and don't have a Flight Mode. Instead, click on each of the Bluetooth and Wi-Fi symbols at the top of the screen and switch them off individually.

Don't leave the laptop chained to the mains

If your laptop spends 95% of its life on your desk, plugged into the mains, you can damage the long-term health of the battery. On the rare occasion you do take the laptop out, you may find its battery indicator trickles down faster than a shot of a particularly potent beverage, or simply lies to you, and runs out of juice when it's reporting that there's still 20% of battery left in the tank.

Some manufacturers ship their laptops with utilities which allow you to alter the battery charge threshold. This, for example, will set the battery to only start charging when below 85% of power and stop at 90%. This will crimp short-term battery life but improve its long-term lifespan. Look for utilities such as HP Support Assistant or Lenovo Vantage that should come pre-installed on your device.

Switch off graphics chips

If you have a laptop with a dedicated graphics chip from Nvidia or AMD, you can fully expect that to hammer your battery life. Most of these laptops will now have an option to switch to so-called integrated graphics, the weaker graphics chips that are bundled in with the main computer processor. Integrated graphics are much kinder on battery life, although they're faintly hopeless for playing the latest 3D games.

If all you're doing is noodling around on the web or watching iPlayer, switch to the integrated graphics and you'll be rewarded with tens of extra battery minutes. Look for the Nvidia or AMD utilities that should come pre-installed on your laptop.

Disconnect peripherals

If you've got anything plugged into your laptop – USB drives, a mouse, your smartphone – they are going to drag down the battery life. Some laptops have a powered USB port for charging mobile phones and other devices, and that really will chew through your battery life, even if you've only connected the phone to transfer photos or videos.

Don't put the laptop directly on your lap

We know, we know… why do they call it a laptop then? However, putting the laptop directly onto your 37°C thighs is going to warm your laptop. That will in due course prompt the laptop's fans to take remedial action (assuming your laptop has fans, of course) and that will take its toll on battery life. Better to put the laptop on a nice cool table. If it's unavoidable to use it on your lap, then put a book, newspaper, or something solid between your legs and the laptop.

Don't push it!

The more strenuous the task you ask your laptop to perform, the harder it has to work and the more battery power it will drink. Among the tasks that are going to sap battery life are 3D gaming, video editing, and photo editing. Watching movies (especially with headphones plugged in), word processing, or browsing the web are much less likely to make the laptop sweat.

CAN I REPLACE MY LAPTOP'S BATTERY?

Ten years ago, this wouldn't have been a problem. Almost every laptop battery could be removed and replaced simply by moving a couple of sliders or undoing a few screws.

Then Mr Steve Jobs pulled a MacBook Air out of a slim brown envelope at an Apple presentation, and ever since the obsession has been with creating wafer-thin sealed units that are impossible for mere mortals to remove the battery from. Laptops do still come with removable batteries, but these are very much in the descendancy, not least because it gives you another reason to buy a new laptop two or three years down the road.

It should be fairly easy to tell if you have a removable battery. Look for clips or a removable section on the base of your laptop. If it's not marked as a removable battery, we strongly suggest you don't take a screwdriver to your laptop and attempt to investigate yourself, unless you're sure of what you're doing. It's very easy to dislodge something from the motherboard and leave yourself with an expensive doorstop.

If you do have a sealed unit, that doesn't mean a battery replacement is out of the question – but we would recommend you take it to a professional repair shop to have it replaced, rather than attempting to do so yourself.

Before you do that, however, get Windows to run a battery report to find out just what kind of state your battery is in. To do this, you need to open something called the Command Prompt in Windows administrator mode. In Windows 10, type 'cmd' into the Windows search menu, right-click on the Command Prompt option that should appear in the search results and choose Run as Administrator. Click Yes on the next screen.

A black window should now appear. In that window, type the command:

powercfg /batteryreport

(Note the space between the g and /)

Hit **ENTER** and Windows should state that a report is saved on a file path that reads something like C:\WINDOWS\system32\ battery-report.html. Copy that entire file path and paste into your web browser's address bar and you can read an incredibly detailed breakdown of your battery's health. It's a godsend for insomniacs.

The key stats to look for are the design capacity and the full charge capacity. If your full charge capacity is only half of the design capacity, it means your laptop's battery life is – at best – half of what it was when the laptop was brand new. Anything less than half signals it's time to consider a replacement battery.

What can I do about it?
- Run a battery report in Windows
- Check to see if your battery is replaceable
- Take a sealed unit for professional replacement

MY COMPUTER SCREEN IS DIRTY – HOW DO I CLEAN IT?

Gone are the days when you could clean a screen with a can of Mr Sheen and a pair of your old pants (everyone did that, right?). Today's computer screens are delicate beasts, often sprayed with a delicate fingerprint-resistant coating that doesn't get on well with abrasive chemicals. So how do you clean a screen of daily detritus without doing damage?

The good news is you don't need any expensive equipment – a cheap microfibre cloth is your friend here. Nor do you necessarily need to invest in these expensive LCD screen sprays that are flogged on Amazon and in computer stores. Most screen spots and smears can be removed by simply damping the cloth with plain water.

First, try cleaning the screen with the dry microfibre cloth. Don't press too hard – this isn't the solid screen of years ago, but a thin layer of glass/plastic with delicate crystals lying just beneath the surface. If you apply too much force, you could permanently damage your screen.

If that doesn't shift all the grime, then lightly dampen the cloth with water and try again. It's vital the cloth isn't so soaked that drips could fall down the screen and into the bezel. Not unless you're keen on the smell of shorted electronics, anyway.

If you need to call in the chemical big guns to shift a stubborn spot, then be super-careful about the screen cleaner you choose. Dell recommends that you don't choose a cleaner with any of the following chemicals for cleaning LCD screens: acetone, ethyl alcohol, toluene, ethyl acid, ammonia, or methyl chloride. If the chemicals used in a cleaner aren't listed, don't use it. You're better off with a slightly dirty screen than one that's had its coating removed by chemicals.

If you're using a cleaning spray, do not squirt it directly on the screen. Spray on the cloth to avoid drips running into the bezels or over the keyboard of a laptop.

What can I do about it?
- Use a microfibre cloth
- Don't spray water/cleaners directly onto the screen
- Don't press too hard

MY COMPUTER'S TOUCHSCREEN HAS STOPPED WORKING!

If your dabs are no longer having the desired effect, and there's no obvious physical damage to your screen, there are several steps you can take to get your touchscreen back into working order.

In our experience, touchscreen failures most often occur after a major update to Windows. Those twice-yearly updates often require new drivers for the touchscreen, which aren't installed until the new version of Windows is in place. If you find your touchscreen has failed after a big Windows refresh, you should first check to see if there are any screen or graphics driver updates available for your device. Your laptop manufacturer might provide a utility that checks for driver updates. Failing that, it's time to dive into the Device Manager.

Search for 'device manager' in Windows search, open the Device Manager from the search results. Now we want to look for two items in particular. First, click on Display Adapters, find the graphics system listed under that tree, right-click on it, and select Update Driver to check if there's any new software available. Repeat that process for 'HID-compliant touch screen', which should be listed under Human Interface Devices. Your computer may need to restart during the installation of graphics drivers or the screen may look weird during the process. Don't panic, it should right itself.

Over-aggressive power management is another potential cause, with Windows deciding to turn the touchscreen element off when the laptop goes to sleep and failing to switch it back on again. This is another Device Manager job. This time, right-click on the 'HID-compliant touch screen' entry, select Properties, and check to see if there's a Power Management tab. If there is, uncheck the box that says 'Allow the computer to turn off this device and save power'.

If new drivers and tweaking the power management don't do the trick, then type 'troubleshooting' into the Windows search bar and see if the operating system can detect any fault with your touchscreen.

Failing that, you might need to circumvent Windows itself. Some laptop manufacturers put a touchscreen diagnostics test into the BIOS of their devices. To access the BIOS, you need to restart the computer and then press a certain key (normally one of the **F** function keys or **ESC**) before Windows boots. A quick Google search (ie. 'Lenovo ThinkPad BIOS key') should reveal the key you need.

Once in the BIOS, look for an entry such as Component Tests (which is the relevant entry for HP laptops, for example). These will ask you to dab the screen and detect if there's a fault with the hardware. If there is, you should be given an error code that will be helpful to your computer manufacturer's helpdesk.

What can I do about it?
- Check for new display/graphics drivers
- Disable touchscreen power management
- Run BIOS diagnostics tests

WHY DOESN'T MY COMPUTER RECOGNISE MY MEMORY CARD?

You've been to a wedding and taken those never-to-be repeated images that you'll cherish for ever. Except your computer is having none of it. Every time you plug the card in, the computer's either acting like it doesn't exist or is throwing up some random error message. Cherish for ever has turned into perish for ever.

Memory cards are sensitive things, which is why professional photographers will use cameras with two memory card slots, one purely acting as a backup for the first.

Part of the problem is the dirt-cheap card readers that are built into most laptops and PCs. These things can corrupt a perfectly good card in no time. Therefore, we'd recommend avoiding card readers as much as possible. Leave the card in the camera, reducing the risk of physical damage as you pop it in and out of the slots, and connect the camera to the computer – either using the supplied USB cable or the Wi-Fi transfer functionality increasingly found on today's digital cameras.

If you've plugged the card into a card reader and now neither the computer nor the camera can see the images stored on it, the card is likely corrupted. The good news is that photos can normally be recovered, even if the computer shrugs its shoulders and says there's no data on the card every time you plug it in.

Memory cards (and any disk drive, for that matter) have the equivalent of a directory or index, which tells the computer where all the images are stored on the card. It's often this index that becomes corrupted, forcing the computer to report that it cannot find any images on the card. The good news is specialist recovery software can still find and restore those images, meaning you should get the vast majority of your images back.

We've used Recuva (**ccleaner.com/recuva**) in the past to rescue images from a defunct memory card. There are free and paid-for versions of the software, but you should be able to pluck files from a duff card without having to using the premium version.

The crucial thing to remember when recovering a memory card is to keep card activity to a minimum, until you can use the recovery software. Don't keep putting the card in new computers, hoping for a miracle – the more the card is accessed, the less chance you have of recovering data. Some sites suggest using Windows' disk recovery tools or even formatting the card! Disk recovery would be our last resort and formatting the card is a guaranteed way to lose all images stored on it!

Generally, when using digital camera memory cards, you should take great care not to remove them while they're being accessed. Always turn the camera off before removing a card and don't yank them out of the computer until you've safely 'ejected' them in Windows. In order to do that, click the up arrow in the little row of icons next to the clock, find Safely Remove Hardware and Eject Media, and then select the memory card for ejection before you pop it out of the reader. This ensures the card isn't being used when it's removed.

We'd also strongly recommend investing in good-quality memory cards from renowned brands such as SanDisk or Samsung. Cheapo cards that you can pick up for a few quid on Amazon or eBay are a false economy.

What can I do about it?

● Keep the card in the camera and transfer images using a cable or Wi-Fi
● Use recovery software such as Recuva to rescue corrupted cards

HOW DO I DEFRAG
MY HARD DISK?

It's 1999. Wi-Fi is still sci-fi, PCs come in any colour as long as it's beige, and Windows is regularly nagging you to defrag your hard disk. Now, 20 years on, how do you perform this once crucial piece of disk maintenance?

First, a look at what disk defragging entails. Think of a hard disk as a grid with millions of little squares. Your hard disk will try to store data sequentially – i.e. if you've got a digital photo stored on the drive, it will attempt to put the bits of data that make up that photo in consecutive slots of the grid.

However, once the disk starts to fill up and bits of data are deleted, bits of files are scattered across the grid. That means the hard disk has to work harder to find all the fragments of data that make up that photo, slowing the computer down.

Defragging tries to clump all the little fragments of files back into adjoining slots on the grid, reducing the amount of time it takes to find all those tiny bits of data and making the computer run more smoothly. Got it? Marvellous.

Now for the good news. You don't need to do this process manually any more. If you search in Windows 7/8/10, you will still find a utility that lets you defrag the hard disk, but it should report that 'scheduled optimisation' is on. Windows handles the process by itself, defragging disks in the background when it detects the data has become scattered.

If you have a solid-state disk (SSD), you might be slightly alarmed that Windows appears to defrag that – conventional wisdom says that it's harmful to defrag them. That might have been true for the very early models, but Windows will now defrag SSDs as part of its routine maintenance to help prolong the life of the drive.

It's generally best not to interfere and simply be glad that this once dull but necessary task has been taken off your schedule.

What can I do about it?
● Nothing – this task is now best left to the operating system!

I'VE RUN OUT OF USB PORTS – WHAT NOW?

In the same way that every household has now run out of plug sockets because everyone is charging their phones, your computer can easily run out of USB sockets for all the different gadgets you want to plug into it. This is a particular problem for laptops, which these days might have as few as one USB port on them! So, what do you do when you run out of ports?

The relatively cheap solution is a USB hub. Much like a wall socket adapter, these convert a single USB port into four, five, six, or more different USB ports, allowing you to use multiple devices from a single USB port on your computer.

However, life is never that straightforward, and there are a few things you need to check before rushing off to order the cheapest hub you can find.

First, note that some USB hubs require external power of their own (i.e. they have to be plugged into the wall power socket). Rule of thumb is the greater the number of USB ports they provide, the greater the chance they'll need their own power source. That means you won't be able to use the hub while using your laptop on a train or plane, for example. Check the specs of a potential purchase very carefully, as these details are often buried deep in the listings.

You also need to make sure you get the right type of USB port. There are now two main types of USB port on computers: Type-A, which are the flat, rectangular ports that have been around for donkey's years and Type-C, which are the much thinner, rounded ports that have become much more commonplace over the past couple of years. Check carefully to make sure you're ordering the right one.

In fact, the Type-C (or USB-C) hubs can be quite complicated, because they can do a lot more than the Type-A. The reason laptops only have one of those ports is because they can carry a lot more data and power. That means a USB-C hub might have connections for an external monitor, SD cards, and regular Type-A and Type-C ports built into the one device.

If you're buying a hub that doesn't require external power, beware that it will output very little power from its own USB ports. If you're looking to charge a phone off your hub, for instance, you'll need to check carefully that it can deliver sufficient juice. Also note that if you're running on laptop battery power, the more devices you plug in, the quicker the battery will drain.

What can I do about it?
- Get a USB hub
- Make sure to buy the right kind (Type-A or Type-C)
- Beware that some require external power

MY PC'S FANS ARE CLOGGED WITH DUST – HOW DO I CLEAN THEM?

If you're looking at the back of your desktop computer and see that the vents have gathered lots of dust, then it's time to act. Blocked fans or limited airflow make your computer much more likely to overheat, and that can lead to sudden crashes, burnt-out components, and expensive repair bills.

However, poor cleaning techniques can also damage those ridiculously sensitive components, so here's how to clean those dust-gubbed fans without making matter worse.

First, let's establish what needs cleaning. On the back of your PC, you'll likely see air-intake vents which may have a case fan directly attached to them. If you open the case, you'll likely see other fans nestled on top of the processor, within a graphics card (if you have one) or dotted around the case. It's a good idea to make sure these are all as free from dust as possible.

Before you start any cleaning, or even open the case to have a look around, you need to make sure you have the right equipment. Anti-static bands are a good idea, as these minimise the chances of you accidentally cooking a component with a build-up of static electricity. If that seems like overkill, make sure you touch a metal part of the outer casing before touching components on the inside, to discharge any static you may have built up, and avoid wearing socks on a carpet while cleaning.

Likewise, make sure the computer is fully unplugged before you start any cleaning work, unless you have a strong desire to spend the rest of your life with charred fingers and Rod Stewart's haircut.

Don't even think about using a vacuum cleaner to remove dust, even a mini one. They will generate static which could definitely do more harm than good. Instead, arm yourself with a can of compressed air (sometimes called 'dust remover'), a clean cloth and some cotton buds.

Use the compressed air to blow dust out of vents and fans, taking care not to blast the air too close to components. Use the cotton buds to remove any stubborn dust from fans blades that won't come loose with air alone.

The cloth comes into play to collect any loose dust that may now have gathered at the bottom of the case. You can dampen the cloth slightly to help pick up the dust, but make sure the cloth isn't wringing wet. The last thing you want is to leave any moisture behind in the PC enclosure. Don't – whatever you do – apply the wet cloth directly to any components.

What can I do about it?

- Take anti-static protection
- Arm yourself with a can of compressed air, cotton buds, and a cloth
- Clean any fans and vents to prevent overheating

WHAT IS THE BLUE SCREEN OF DEATH?

You may have heard of the Blue Screen of Death – it's normally the last thing you see before putting your fist through said screen.

Blue Screens of Death (BSOD to the techy elite, who love to initialise everything) are rare these days, but they do still occur. So, what are they and what do you do when you're confronted by one?

A Blue Screen of Death is a hard crash in Windows. It takes the form of a blue screen (hence the name, kids) and an often-indecipherable error message. You won't get a chance to save your work or close the error message and go about your business, because the crash is so monumental that Windows needs to restart itself.

Before it does, however, try to take note of any error message code that is printed on the screen. If you've got a smartphone in your pocket, take a quick snap of the screen so that you can Google the error code later. Blue screens are generally nothing to worry about – they happen to the best of us from time to time – but the error message might give you a clue as to what went wrong and how to avoid such crashes happening in the future, so do your best to get that code. You've got to be quick, as it will disappear after a few seconds.

Nine times out of ten, a computer will recover itself from a Blue Screen of Death and carry on as if nothing ever happened. If you had unsaved changes in a Word document or Excel spreadsheet, reopen the application and look to see if you're offered the chance to recover a document. This will normally appear in a pane on the left-hand side of the application. If it doesn't appear automatically, click File, then Open, and scroll to the bottom of the screen and click the button that says Recover Unsaved Documents. Word/Excel takes regular snapshots of work in progress and saves them to a temporary files folder, which might save your bacon if you've forgotten to hit the Save button for the past couple of hours.

If the computer continues to blue screen, something more serious is afoot. Faulty or outdated graphics drivers are a problem that often leads to a BSOD, so go into the Windows Device Manager, find the Display Adapters section, right-click on your graphics card/chip, and select Update Driver. Windows will search for a new version of the graphics card's software and install any updates it can find online.

What can I do about it?
- Make a quick note of any error message
- Google that error code to find out what caused the crash
- Update graphics drivers if Blue Screens of Death are persistent

WHY CAN'T MY COMPUTER SEE MY PRINTER?

Your PC is connected to the Wi-Fi network; your printer is connected to the Wi-Fi network. But can you get A to see B? Can you heck. Here's how to deal with a printer that has seemingly gone AWOL.

The first thing to check is that your printer and PC are actually connected to the same network and both devices are turned on. Some dual-band Wi-Fi routers offer two networks you can connect to at home – one on the 2.4GHz band and one on the 5GHz band. Most devices will still detect another device on a different band, but just to make sure, connect them to the same band. (See our question on why your computer can't see devices on your Wi-Fi network on page 75 for more.)

If both are definitely connected to the same band, then it's time to dive into Window's settings. Type 'printer' into the Windows search bar and open the Printers & Scanners menu that appears. If your printer isn't listed on that screen, press 'Add a printer or scanner' and try to find it that way.

If your printer is listed, but there's a little grey 'offline' label underneath it, we need to dig a little deeper. Click on the printer and select Manage. If this is your primary printer, press the Set As Default button – this can sometimes be enough to make Windows rediscover the printer and make them best of friends from here on in.

If not, click on the Run The Troubleshooter link on that page. Windows will now perform a series of network tests to try to connect to your absent paper-spewer.

If that still doesn't deliver any joy, go back a screen, click on the printer again, and select Remove Device. This will uninstall the printer completely. Reboot your computer and then try adding the printer afresh.

On a Mac, you'll find the printer settings by clicking on the Apple in the top left of the screen, selecting System Preferences, and choosing the Printers & Scanners option. If your printer isn't already shown in the list on the left, click the + button under the list. You can also change the default printer from this screen, if more than one is installed on your Mac.

What can I do about it?

- Check the printer and computer are on the same wireless band
- Set the printer as the default printer in Windows/Mac
- Run the printer troubleshooter

WHY CAN'T MY COMPUTER SEE OTHER DEVICES ON MY WI-FI NETWORK?

You've got two devices both claiming to be connected to your home Wi-Fi, and yet when you try and access a printer, a NAS drive, a smartphone or some other device via your computer, your PC simply refuses to see it. Short of waving the device in front of the computer's webcam and screaming 'can you see it now!', how do you get out of this conundrum?

One reason for this can be devices accessing different Wi-Fi bands on the same router. Confused already? Fetch a cup of tea and let us explain.

Most modern Wi-Fi routers are dual-band. That means they operate at two frequencies: one in the 2.4GHz band and one in the less congested 5GHz band. Most routers won't make this visible to the end user. Your Wi-Fi network will be called something like 'Dave's Home Wi-Fi' and the router will allocate devices to different bands automatically.

However, that can sometimes mean devices on the 2.4GHz band can't 'see' devices connected to the 5GHz band. It shouldn't happen, but it occasionally does. BT Home Hubs, we're staring long and hard at you.

One way to sidestep this problem is to make your router give each band a separate name. So, instead of 'Dave's Home

Wi-Fi', you could have 'Dave's Home Wi-Fi 2.4' and 'Dave's Home Wi-Fi 5', for instance. That way, you can be sure both devices are connected to the same band and so should be able to interact with one another.

Instructions on how to set this up vary from router to router. On a BT Smart Hub, for instance, you need to access the router's settings from a web browser. This will normally be an IP address such as http://192.168.1.254. Google the name of your router and 'IP address' to find yours. To access the management settings, you'll also need the router's admin password, which is normally printed somewhere on the router itself. Once you're in there, look for a setting that allows you to separate bands – it may well be in the advanced settings.

If that still doesn't work, you might try assigning the other device (printer, smartphone etc.) a static IP address on your network. Every device on your network will be given an IP address by the router every time it connects; however, that address can change because the default behaviour is for addresses to be 'dynamically' assigned each time. That can cause problems when your computer tries to find the device and it's no longer at that address.

The way to solve that is to tell the router to give your printer, for example, the same address every time it connects. Again, open your router's settings and look for a section that lists the devices currently connected. Now click on the relevant device and you should find an option to 'always use this IP address' or something similar. You shouldn't need to do this for every device, but it's worth trying if you've got a problem device that your computer refuses to see.

What can I do about it?

- Separate your Wi-Fi bands and make sure both devices connect to the same band
- Assign problem devices a static IP address

MY COMPUTER HAS BROKEN AFTER A WINDOWS UPDATE. WHAT NOW?

Nothing is more likely to send a Windows computer owner into a fit of apoplectic rage than Windows Update. Not only does it inevitably kick in at the worst possible time, but it can sometimes leave your PC in a crumpled pile, incapable of displaying anything other than an error message. So much for progress, eh?

If your PC has problems after a Windows Update, there are several steps you can take to get things back in working order.

If the computer can still boot into the Windows desktop, but has some minor ailment that you can't resolve – loss of audio, refusal to see external hard disks, graphics glitches – then turning back the clock is often the easiest way out.

You have two choices here. You can uninstall the update and roll back to the previous version. If you type 'Windows Update' into the Windows search bar, open the Windows Update Settings, and you've installed the update in the past week, you should see the option here to roll back. If not, click on View Update History and select the Uninstall Updates option from this screen, then select the most recent Windows Update.

The other, and normally safer, option is to use the System Restore facility. This rolls back Windows to a certain point in time, but you have to have this feature turned on beforehand (it should be on by default if you've never fiddled with it). Type 'System Restore' into Windows search, click on Create A Restore Point, and then click on the System Restore button. Follow the instructions on screen and hopefully you should be presented with the option to restore the computer to a time before the update was applied. This process can take a while and may see the computer restart itself a few times. Try not to panic and let it run its course.

If an uninstallation/roll back does the trick, the next job is to prevent Windows automatically installing the faulty update once more. In the Windows Update settings screen we mentioned above, you should see an option to pause updates for seven days. Hit that and hope Microsoft fixes any flawed updates in the intervening period. To be fair to Microsoft, it's normally pretty good at patching borked updates promptly.

If the Windows Update flaw is so bad that your computer refuses to get to the Windows desktop or displays a Blue Screen of Death message every time you attempt to fire it up, then it's time for a little intensive care.

With a bit of luck, after a couple of failed attempts to boot, Windows 10 will throw itself into the blue troubleshooting screen, from where you want to click on Advanced Options. Here you have the option to attempt a Start-Up Repair, where Windows will attempt to fix itself. If that doesn't work, that screen also contains options to Uninstall Updates and System Restore, which should be your next ports of call.

If you're still snookered, it's time for more drastic action. You may have to try to boot Windows from installation media. Almost nobody has discs these days, so you will need to download a Windows installation to a USB drive and repair your computer from that. See the question on 'How do I reinstall Windows 10?' on page 100 for precise instructions.

What can I do about it?

- Roll back or uninstall the updates
- Use System Restore to return to a working configuration
- Block broken updates from re-installing
- Use the troubleshooting settings to repair a system that won't start

WHY HAS MY LAPTOP SCREEN GONE VERY DIM?

If your laptop screen is suddenly dimmer than the average reality TV contestant, the solution is likely to be searingly simple or a complete pain in the hard drives. This is one of those problems with no middle ground.

First, let's deal with the easy ones. Your laptop should have screen brightness controls somewhere on the keyboard – look for two symbols that look like suns, often on the row of **F** numbers at the top. You may need to press the **Fn** button along with the relevant icon to make the screen brighter or dimmer.

If your screen is dim when you're running on battery power, that's what meant to happen. Windows' power management settings reduce screen brightness to save batteries when you're unchained from the mains, but if the screen dimming is too aggressive you can change that. Type 'battery saver' into the Windows 10 search bar and open the Battery Saver Settings. In there you should find a box ticked that says 'Lower screen brightness while in battery saver'. Untick that, but beware that your battery life will be shortened as a result.

Some fancier laptops have dynamic brightness, which use sensors to detect the level of ambient light and adjust brightness accordingly. Normally, this is a good thing, but we've seen it behave erratically on some models.

If you wish to turn this off, first unplug the laptop from the power adapter, and then open the Windows Control Panel (search for it if you don't know where it lives). In Control Panel, search for Power Options, then click Change Plan Settings. On the next screen, select the advanced settings option and then click the + sign next to Display. You should see an Adaptive Brightness setting here, which you can switch off.

If your screen hasn't so much dimmed, but gone a funny yellow colour, you may have accidentally activated the night mode. This is a relatively new feature in PCs and Macs that is meant to reduce the amount of blue light belting out of your screen, which has been linked with sleeplessness. In Windows, night mode can be deactivated by clicking on the speech bubble-like icon in the bottom-right corner of the screen and selecting the Night Light icon. On a Mac, click the Apple menu, select System Preferences, select the Display icon, click on the Night Shift tab and select 'Off' from the schedule drop-down menu.

If the screen is very dark, almost impossible to see in a normal room, then there's a chance the backlight has failed. That's a problem that nobody but the most technically competent tinkerer is going to solve themselves, so it's time for a visit to the repair shop.

What can I do about it?

- Adjust the power management settings
- Turn off adaptive brightness
- Make sure you're not in night mode

WHY WON'T THE EXTERNAL SCREEN PLUGGED INTO MY LAPTOP WORK?

The problem with laptop screens is – unless you've bought a supertanker of a laptop – the display is pretty small. Which is why many people will choose to plug it into a bigger screen if they're using the laptop at their desk. But what happens when you bung the cord in the port and no picture appears on your external screen?

Windows and macOS should both automatically recognise when an external screen is plugged in and show the desktop. However, if that doesn't happen, you can try a little manual prompting. On Windows, press the ⊞ **Windows** key and **P** simultaneously to bring up the display options, which include the options to extend the display across both screens, mirror what appears on both screens, or have either screen turned off and just use the other.

On a Mac, click the Apple symbol in the top-left corner, choose System Preferences, and then Displays. Here you'll find similar options to mirror, extend, and so forth.

If the computer still doesn't acknowledge you've got a second screen connected, check the cable is plugged in firmly at both ends and that the power to the monitor is switched on. Change the cable to rule out any chance of a wiring fault.

If you're connecting a monitor via one of the more modern USB-C ports, you first need to check that the port is capable of carrying display information. Check to see if the port is marked with a little screen or lightning icon. If the ports aren't marked, try plugging the USB-C cable into another USB-C port on the computer to see if that does the trick.

A faulty Windows display driver can prevent external screens from being recognised by the computer. To check your drivers are fully up to date, open the Device Manager by searching for it in the Windows search bar. Click on the little arrow next to Display Adapters and right-click on Update Driver. Windows will now scour the internet for an updated version of your driver. Screens can go blank or display fuzzy images while display drivers are being updated and installed, so don't panic if that happens – just let Windows finish the job and all should right itself in the end.

What can I do about it?
- Check the Windows/Mac display settings
- Make sure cables are plugged into correct port if using USB-C
- Update the display drivers

WHY IS MY COMPUTER SO SLOW?

If we had a quid for every time we'd been asked this question, we'd be sipping cocktails on a beach in Bermuda. Like all of us, computers tend to slow with age, but problems can also come on suddenly which turn a once nimble computer into a lumbering sloth.

Here we are going to run through some – but by no means an exhaustive list – of the problems that can cause a computer to operate on a go-slow, and tell you how to fix them.

Too many programs loading at startup

One common cause of Windows seemingly taking an age to get ready after you've pressed the power button is that you've got too much software loading in the background every time the computer starts. This is categorically not your fault, but the fault of thoughtless software developers, who program their apps to run at startup, often without any just cause.

Fortunately, it's much easier to eject software from the startup routine than it used to be. Type the word 'start' into the Windows 10 search menu and click on the Startup Apps setting. You should now be presented with a list of all the apps that are activated to fire up when you first switch on your PC. Switch off any that have no right to be there or apps that you barely ever use.

Note that there are some apps that you definitely shouldn't prevent running at startup, including antivirus software, online storage systems such as Dropbox, and utilities that control your wireless mouse and keyboard.

Running out of storage space

A computer that is running close to its storage limit is likely to run very slowly indeed, particularly if that storage is a conventional hard disk. Windows uses spare storage space as a temporary replacement for memory (RAM). But if there's no spare storage, it cannot do that, slowing the PC down. A close-to-capacity hard disk also has to work much harder, meaning the computer will be slower to load software or access files.

It's important, therefore, not to let your PC get clogged with files. If your main disk is more than 90% full, it's time for a clear-out.

Windows has a few tools that can help you clear space. If you type 'apps' into the Windows search bar and click on Add or Remove Programs, you'll get a list of all the software stored on your PC. Use the drop-down menu to sort that list by size and then get rid of any space-hungry software that you no longer use.

If you type 'storage' into the search menu, you should also find Windows' storage settings. Here you can turn on an option called Storage Sense, which keeps an eye on folders that tend to gather unnecessary clutter, such as the temporary files and recycle bin. It can also delete previous versions of Windows that remain on the system, although this does prevent you turning the clock back if a Windows Update borks your PC (see our separate question on how to recover from faulty Windows updates, page 78).

The Downloads folder – where Windows stores all the stuff you download off the internet – is another prime culprit for collecting files that you no longer need. You should find a link to the Downloads folder in the Quick Access section on the left of the window, when you open Windows Explorer.

Your system is riddled with malware

PC pestilence is a common cause of computer go-slows. You've been clicking on everything you see on the internet again, haven't you?

Even in 2020, it's still woefully easy to download one delicious-looking free utility and get three or four more sneakily bundled into the same package. Ironically, this often happens with free apps that claim to boost the performance of your PC.

These applications often install adware, which sits in the background, frequently blotting your screen with pop-up ads. They install browser toolbars that similarly plague you with ads or redirect your search engine to some awful alternative. Or these apps sit invisibly in the background, either hoovering up your personal data to sell to the highest bidder or running programs that generate bitcoins (a virtual currency) for their masters.

This stuff can sometimes be tricky to spot and even harder to remove. The developers don't tend to call this stuff BIG NASTY MALWARE that you can easily remove from Add/Remove Programs. Make sure your security software is regularly set to fully scan your system, not just perform a quick scan every now and then.

If you see a piece of software installed on your system and you're not sure what it is, bang its name into Google. Sites such as **shouldiremoveit.com** are also very handy at separating the wheat from the chaff and identifying rogue files that have slipped on to your system.

Golden rule: if you're not sure what something is, don't install it in the first place. And don't just blithely click Next or OK when installing new software. Take your time, read the screens carefully, and make sure you're not getting more than you bargained for.

Too many or rogue browser tabs
If you check the Task Manager (press **CTRL+ALT+DELETE** simultaneously on Windows systems), chances are you'll find it's

the web browser that's hogging most of your computer's memory – especially if you've got loads of browser tabs open.

Some browsers are better than others at managing memory. Some shove unused tabs into the background, others don't, meaning those 20 tabs you've got open while researching that weekend break to Paris are breaking your computer. It's generally best to close any tabs you're not using to prevent them gobbling up spare memory that could be better used for the stuff you're actually viewing.

Rogue tabs are another problem. This normally occurs on sites where you're not just looking at a static webpage, but doing something such as word processing, playing video, or even running a game in the web browser. These web apps can swallow memory, bringing the rest of the computer down with them. A key sign this is happening are browser warnings that a 'site is not responding'. Sometimes you can wait for these temporary glitches to resolve; other times you have to shut down the tab.

Browsers now have their own task managers to help you root out the rogue tabs. In Chrome, you'll find it by pressing the **SHIFT** and **ESC** keys simultaneously, in Firefox you can access the task manager by typing 'about:performance' into the address bar. These let you kill tabs that are taking way more than their fair share of memory.

You're in the wrong power mode

Windows has different power modes for different scenarios. If you're running a laptop on battery power, for instance, Windows will put the device in a battery-saving mode that throttles the processor and reduces background activity so that the computer doesn't get so hot, fire up the fans, and canter through the battery.

It is possible that this setting has been accidentally activated even when the laptop is plugged in and can cope with running at full throttle. To check, plug the laptop in and then click on the tiny power socket/battery icon that's in the row of icons next to the clock. You should be presented with a slider, ranging from Best Battery Life to Best Performance. Drag it to Best Performance if it's not already there.

You've just installed a major Windows update

Every six months or so, Windows 10 is given a major new update. These are the ones that tend to take an age to download/install and change the appearance of Windows ever so slightly.

After installing one of these, you may notice that Windows is particularly sluggish for a day or so. This is normally down to Windows rebuilding its search index in the background, and there's not much you can do about it, except let it runs its course. (It can be wise to leave the computer on overnight to let it complete the job while you're not actively using it – assuming you're not an insomniac or a security guard.)

What's the Windows search index? Every file stored on your computer has to be scanned and indexed so that when (in theory) you search for a keyword in one of your documents, Windows returns the correct file in its search results. Every time Windows installs a major new version, that index has to be recreated from scratch, for reasons that aren't entirely clear. It's one of those pain points that we just have to deal with.

Your computer is getting on a bit

Just as when you get to 40, your Park Run times tend to slope towards a Park Walk, so too your computer's performance is going to suffer with age.

There are several contributory factors here. Windows/macOS tends to get a bit heavier with every update; so too do all the applications stored on your computer, making it harder for your once sprightly computer to keep up. There's also an accumulation of digital cruft over time that can lead even high-performance PCs to struggle after three or four years.

Windows 10 has an excellent option to 'reset' your PC that can counter this problem. This will effectively wipe the PC clean and start afresh, but leaves all your documents, photos, and other files intact. Despite this promise, make sure you have a backup of all that personal data in case anything goes wrong during the process. You will need to reinstall all the software on your PC, so make sure you've either got the disks handy or know which website to download the software from.

Type 'reset' into Windows search to find this option.

WHY IS THE INTERNET SO SLOW ON MY COMPUTER?

This is one of those questions that has a million different potential answers, but when people make this complaint it's usually because surfing the web or downloading movies is much slower than they expect it to be. They've paid the man for an ultrafast broadband connection and feel like they're getting one powered by a hamster wheel. Let's deal with the most likely causes.

First, you need to ascertain whether it's the internet connection itself that's at fault. To start with, we want to check something called the sync speed of your connection, which you can normally find by delving into your router's settings. On a BT Hub, for instance, type 192.168.1.254 into a web browser's address bar, then click the Status option and you should get a sync speed readout. If your download (or downstream) sync speed is reporting as, say, 5Mbits/sec and you're paying for an 80Mbits/sec connection, it's time for a word with your broadband provider's support team, as your connection isn't delivering the promised speeds.

If your sync speed is roughly what you're paying for (it may be a little less, but don't lose too much sleep over that), then there's likely something going wrong in between your router and computer. One way to test if it's the computer or router to blame is to run a couple of speed tests. Download Ookla's free speedtest app on your phone or tablet and take a speed reading. Now go to **speedtest.net** on your computer and repeat the process. Try to take both tests while nobody else in the house is downloading massive files or doing anything demanding (such as streaming video) over the connection.

If the speed test results from your computer are much slower than from the mobile device, that suggests a problem with the computer. If both mobile and computer are much slower than the sync speed, then it's more likely a problem with the router.

Dealing with router problems is a little beyond the remit of this book (we're not paid overtime, you know). But common router issues include poorly configured signal boosters, poor placement of the router, interference from nearby electrical devices, or simply running on very old router equipment that cannot cope with today's speeds.

If the fault's with the computer, there are a few things to check. The most obvious is signal strength and location of the computer. If you're using it in a loft extension or back bedroom that's a few solid brick walls away from the router, it may be that the wireless connection simply isn't strong enough. You can get a rough guide of how good the signal is by clicking on the little Wi-Fi symbol next to the clock on a PC or in the bar at the top of the screen on a Mac. If the symbol next to your router's name is not solid white/black, but showing greys, then you might well have a signal problem.

If it's a laptop, does the speed improve if you move to another room closer to the router? If it's a desktop PC, a powerline signal booster placed halfway between the router and the computer might help. It's normally best to buy signal boosters that are the same make as your router, but most should work fine and they're not very expensive – around £30 for a unit from reputable firms such as TP-Link or Netgear.

It's also possible there's a problem with the wireless radio inside your computer. Wireless software drivers are frequently updated, so check that you've got the latest version of those or that there's not a problem with your existing drivers. Use the Windows search facility to find the Device Manager, click on the little arrow next to Network Adapters and look for a wireless card made by a company such as Intel or Broadcom. Right-click on that and select Update Driver to make sure everything is bang up to date.

It's entirely possible that the router is syncing at the right speed, the speed test results are fine, but surfing the internet still feels like you're wading through porridge. In which case, the problem is likely to be activity on the computer itself.

Malware can sit in the background, using your internet connection to do stuff such as 'mining' the virtual Bitcoin currency, which can hamper the perceived speed of the internet connection. More obviously, toolbars and adware that you've inadvertently downloaded onto your computer can cause the web browser to crawl. Go into your browser's settings and check the add-ons or extensions menu for things you don't want or need and disable them.

What can I do about it?
- Check your router is syncing at the correct speed
- Take speed tests on different devices
- Check the wireless signal
- Update the wireless drivers on your computer

WHY IS MY COMPUTER MAKING A SCRATCHING NOISE?

There are two possible explanations for this. Either a mouse has found a way inside your computer – and we're not talking about the thing that moves the cursor – or your hard disk is in grave danger of failure.

A hard disk is a bit like a vinyl record player, except the heads hover over the platter when reading data instead of a needle physically dropping onto the disk like they do with an LP. When a hard disk starts making a scratching or grinding sound, it's normally a sign that the heads are coming into contact with those highly sensitive glass platters and that's very bad news indeed. Terminal, in fact.

If you're a wise owl, your computer will be backed up on a daily basis, meaning any data loss should be minimal. If you've taken a more laissez-faire attitude to backups, then you're in something of a bind.

The longer you leave that computer running, the more chance you have of causing permanent damage to those hard disk platters and all that data being lost forever. However, unless you've got a clean lab, a degree in mechanical engineering, and several grands' worth of specialist equipment in your back bedroom, you're unlikely to be able to recover the data yourself anyway.

Instead, if you want those photos of last summer's holiday to Tenerife back, you're going to need to send the hard disk to data recovery specialists such as Seagate or Ontrack. We'll warn you now, you'll likely be looking at a bill that runs well into the hundreds of pounds to recover the data and have it sent back to you on a new hard disk.

The moral of the story is, of course, to always keep backups. Hopefully you read this sentence before something goes wrong...

What can I do about it?

- Switch off the computer immediately
- Rely on your data backups and replace the disk, or...
- ...send the broken disk to a data recovery specialist

I'VE FORGOTTEN MY WINDOWS 10 PASSWORD – HOW DO I GET INTO MY COMPUTER?

Memory is a funny thing. You can remember every lyric to *Glad That I Live Am I* that was drummed into you at school assemblies, but you can't remember the Windows password that YOU REALLY NEED NOW.

If you've been struck down by a nasty case of password amnesia, we'll show you how to recover your password and then make sure you're never caught out again.

The good news is that Windows 10 passwords are these days normally linked to Microsoft accounts. In other words, you use your Microsoft email address and password to log in to Windows. That means you can use the online password recovery tools to set a new password and get yourself back into Windows, provided your computer is connected to the internet and can receive the new password.

The Microsoft account recovery page can be found at: **account.live.com/password/reset**.

If you've managed to avoid Windows' nagging and not use a Microsoft account as your Windows login, but have instead set a local username and password, you can still get back in. On the login screen, click the Reset Password link. You will be asked to answer a security question that you've provided the answer to previously. That should sneak you back under the gates.

If you've failed both the password and security question tests, things become trickier. First, check to see if you've previously set up any alternative login methods: fingerprint, PIN number, face recognition etc. These will be offered under the Sign-In Options link that appears on the login screen. We'll talk more about these in a moment.

If not, pray that someone else in your household has an administrator account on the same PC. They can then use this account to reset your password. If not, you're now in a world of pain. You may well have to reset the PC entirely, but that will take all your data and installed applications with it. If you're properly backed up, that might not be much more than a minor inconvenience. If you're not properly backed up and the data on your hard disk isn't encrypted, you (or a PC technician) might be able to recover the data before you fully reset the PC as a last resort.

How do you avoid this happening again? As we mentioned above, Windows 10 now offers a range of login options. If your laptop has a fingerprint reader, you can log in with the dab of a digit. If it has a fancy webcam, you may be able to use facial recognition to automatically log you in when you plonk yourself in front of the screen. On any device, you can use a PIN instead of a password. Any of these will get you into your system if you forget your main Windows password. To set these up, type 'sign in' into the Windows 10 search bar and click the Sign-In Options setting, then follow the on-screen instructions.

Another great tool to have in your locker is a password manager. These store the gazillions of passwords we all need to log in to various websites and services these days, and they create strong, unique passwords that you don't have to remember yourself. All you have to remember is the password for the password manager itself, although you can often use a fingerprint reader on your smartphone to unlock a password manager's app.

Note that no password manager will automatically fill in your Windows password, like it will on any of the websites that you visit. However, you can manually store your Windows password in the password manager, so that if you ever forget it, you can log in to the app on your phone and retrieve the password.

There are many password managers out there, but we'd recommend the free BitWarden (**bitwarden.com**), which works on practically any device you can think of and is both powerful but simple to use.

What can I do about it?

- Use the Microsoft Account recovery website
- Try an alternative login method (if previously set up)
- Use another admin account on the same PC

MY COMPUTER IS HORRIBLY SLOW. HOW DO I REINSTALL WINDOWS 10?

In the bad old days, people used to recommend users reinstall Windows every 12–18 months, just to blow away the Windows cobwebs and make the system feel sprightly again. Modern Windows is much better at not gradually amassing clutter, but if you've been struck by a virus, hit an inexplicable performance problem (don't worry, chaps, it happens to the best of us), or simply want to wipe the slate clean and start with a fresh system, then reinstalling Windows still has benefits.

The good news is it's much easier to do these days. And that's largely down to a feature introduced with Windows 10 called Reset Your PC. Instead of wiping out the whole system and starting again, as if you've just got the system home from the shop, Reset leaves your personal files intact but clears out all the software you have installed on the PC. This should (and normally does) return the PC to full health, whilst saving you the bother of having to restore all of your documents, photos, and Status Quo MP3s from a backup.

That said… always, always, always take a full backup before performing any Reset or reinstall procedure. Things can go wrong. If you don't take a backup, it will go wrong. It is known.

So, how do you perform a Reset? If you can still get to the Windows 10 desktop, type 'reset' into the Windows search bar and select the option that says Reset This PC. On the screen that appears, hit Get Started under the Reset This PC section and follow the on-screen instructions. You'll get two options – one that leaves your personal files intact and one that removes absolutely everything. The latter is a good option if you're donating the PC to a friend or family member and don't want them poking through your holiday photos, for example.

The Reset can take a while and your PC may restart several times during the process. Resist the temptation to press the power button and start again if you think it's got stuck – that will normally end in tears.

If your computer won't boot to the Windows desktop, you might be able to use the recovery tools to Reset the PC. When you first power up the computer, look for a message that tells you which key to press to interrupt the normal startup – it varies from system to system, but it's normally something like **ESC**, **ENTER**, or one of the **F** function keys.

When you've entered that menu, look for an option to recover your computer and then, under the troubleshooting menu, you should find the option to Reset your PC. It will work as above.

If you can't even get to that screen, a full reinstall might be in order. To do this you're going to need a sizeable USB memory stick (at least 8GB) and another computer. Go to the Microsoft website at **bit.ly/32sColv** and follow the instructions for downloading and installing the Windows 10 installation media on another PC.

Once that process has completed, you need to plug that USB drive into your broken computer and hopefully it will boot into the Windows setup tool. If it doesn't, switch the PC off and on again and try entering the BIOS menu (Google your computer's model name and 'BIOS key' to find out which key does this). Look for boot or startup options and then select removable USB drive as the device to boot from first. Restart the PC and it should boot from the USB drive.

Note, this reinstallation process will wipe everything from your PC and give you a completely clean install. If there are photos, documents, or other vital files on that PC that you don't have backed up, then it's worth seeking professional help to see whether you can recover that data before wiping and starting afresh.

What can I do about it?
- Backup the PC (if possible)
- Reset the PC from within Windows or the recovery tools
- Reinstall Windows from a USB stick if the above won't work

WHY HAVE ALL THE ICONS ON MY WINDOWS DESKTOP GONE MISSING?

Nothing inspires a quick bout of panic quite as much as switching on your PC to find all the icons you had carefully arranged on your desktop have gone walkabout. Obviously, it's nice to get a clear view of your computer wallpaper, but WHERE ARE MY ICONS?

Calm down. This is a normally an easy one to solve and you won't have lost anything.

Drag the mouse pointer to any clear space on the Windows desktop and right-click. Select View and, in the drop-down menu that appears, look for an option that says Show Desktop Icons. If there's not a tick next to it, then click on that option and your icons should magically pop back into place.

If it's not all of your desktop icons that have gone astray but one in particular, open the Recycle Bin and look for the missing item. You can search for it by name using the search box in the top-right of the window. If it was a shortcut to a program, rather than a document or photo, search for 'shortcut' and you should get a list of all the deleted shortcuts.

If you need to create a new program shortcut on your desktop, search for the program in the Windows search bar, and then drag the program from the Start menu to the desktop, where a new shortcut (or link, as Windows now seems to call it) will be created.

If an icon's image has gone walkabout, try right-clicking on an empty space on the desktop and selecting Refresh – this redraws the page and will hopefully return the icon back to its former glory.

What can I do about it?

- Right-click on desktop, select View, and then Show Desktop Icons
- Look for missing icons in Recycle Bin
- Create a new shortcut by dragging from Start menu

10 WAYS YOU CAN BREAK YOUR COMPUTER ALL BY YOURSELF

1. Not uninstalling programs properly

There is a way to uninstall software from a Windows computer, and that way is NOT to navigate to the Program Files folder on your C: drive and delete the folder of the app in question. That's the way to leave a whole heap of files behind and be forced to dismiss error messages every time you switch on your computer. Search 'remove programs' in the Windows search bar and use the Add/Remove Programs facility to uninstall software properly. Your computer is not an iPad, so you need to do it this longer way around.

2. Turning on very cold laptops

This is a peculiarly British problem, but we've lost count of the number of times we've seen people take a laptop out of their bag on a bitterly cold day and then switch it on immediately. That's a guaranteed way to generate condensation on your screen and the internal components – computers and moisture are not a good mix. Leave the laptop to acclimatise to room temperature for 10–15 minutes before switching it on.

3. Downloading 'freebies' from dodgy sites

Everyone loves a freebie and there's plenty of good, reputable free software out there. But there's an awful lot of shysterware too, which installs spyware, adware, or unwanted applications on your machine with it. Don't download just anything you find online and assume your security software will take care of any nastiness (see point 6). Check reviews, Google the software's name, and make sure you know what you're downloading on your PC before you press the Install button.

4. Answering a phone call from Microsoft

'Hello, I'm calling from Microsoft's support team, we have a discovered a virus on your computer.' No, no you haven't. What you have discovered is a way to con people into installing software on their PC which will eventually rob them blind. If you get a phone call from Microsoft, your broadband provider, or anyone else trying to convince you to install some software or to visit a certain website, hang up. Legitimate companies simply do not make these calls.

5. Installing fix-it utilities

Your computer is running so slowly, you're beginning to look longingly at abacuses. Naturally enough, you download a Guaranteed To Make Your Computer 634% Faster application over the internet... and it's made your PC even slower than it was in the first place. Most fix-it utilities aren't worth the time of day. Most will simply repeat jobs that the operating system does already, some will make your PC worse. Think of a phrase involving barge poles and apply.

6. Run without security software

You may think you're smart enough not to open iffy attachments or visit dodgy websites, and are thus immune from malware, but this isn't 1998. Malware has evolved to the point where you don't need to do something actively dumb to get yourself infected. Even reputable websites can have code injected into their ads that infect your PC, without them or you ever knowing. Windows 10 has baked-in security software that's perfectly fine and doesn't slow your PC. Don't be a spanner and switch it off.

7. Powering down during Windows updates

This isn't as critical as it used to be – Microsoft has built tools that can recover an interrupted update – but it's still far from a good idea to power down the computer during an update. Don't be fooled by a progress bar that hasn't moved in a good while. Knotty parts of an update can take a while and leave you staring at messages such as '83% installed' for half an hour or so. Only if there's no movement for hours on end, should you bite the bullet and press the power button. Laptop users – make sure you're plugged in before starting an update and don't pull the cord until it's done.

8. Tinkering with the Registry

There are a lot on online advice sites that will show you how to solve problems by editing the Windows Registry. The Registry is a database of configuration settings and it's not something that should be meddled with lightly, because if you mess something up here, Windows itself might not start. If you're confident you know what you're doing, at least make sure you take a backup of the Registry, so that if something does go skew-whiff, you can put it back.

9. Getting in over your head

Computers are complex beasts. Even (ahem) internationally renowned tech book authors sometimes look at a screen, scratch their head, and slide off to the pub. The general rule of thumb is that if you don't know what you're doing, don't fiddle with it. The 'what harm can it do?' attitude has borked many a good computer. Professional help is often cheaper than a new PC.

10. Giving the kids admin rights

It's dead easy to set up different user accounts on a PC – just search for 'add user' in the Windows search bar and follow the instructions. Don't let kids roam on the same account you use, as the main account has admin rights, allowing you to install software, meddle with settings, even reset the whole PC. When you try and add a Windows 10 account, you'll be asked if it's for an adult or a child – select child and you can limit which apps they can use, set screen-time limits, and generally keep the PC-wreckers under control.

HOW DO I MAKE MY LAPTOP FANS LESS NOISY?

When you're in the zone and trying to bash out the final, say, 15,000 words of a book that has to be in next week (gulp), the last thing you want is the distraction of your laptop fans wheezing like Hal with a heavy cold. But there are safe ways to banish that fan noise and not-so-safe methods. Here's how to do it.

One of the easiest ways to cut down on the fan noise is to change your power plan. We mentioned this before in the section about 'why is my computer so slow' (see page 85), but this time we're using the power plan to crimp performance when the laptop is plugged in instead of boosting it.

Why? Well, 90% of what most people do on their computer doesn't require maximum processing power. Web browsing, word processing, the odd email doesn't need the processor running at full pelt, which heats up the system and forces the fans to kick in. To change the power mode in Windows, click on the little plug/battery icon in the bottom right-hand corner, and move the slider from 'Best performance' to 'Better performance'. If you're doing some heavy lifting – such as video editing or gaming – you can always move it back, but if you want to hear less fan noise, this is one way to achieve it.

Another way to limit fan noise is to change what the laptop is placed upon. Your lap is, ironically, about the worst place for it, because your thighs are two massive heat conductors (yes, we say that to all the girls). Likewise, don't place the laptop on a quilt, sofa, or any other insulating surface.

There are cheap (sub £20) stands that you can buy for laptops which lift the base off a flat surface, improving the airflow and not blocking any vents that may reside on the base of your laptop. They might be worth a shot if you're constantly battling fan noise and often use your laptop at a desk.

One trick we would definitely not recommend is to use software to reduce your fan speed. There are apps such as SpeedFan (Windows) and smcFanControl (Mac) that you can use to manually control the speed of your fans. However, these are intended for enthusiast tinkerers, the kind of people who 'overclock' the speed of their processors to eke out maximum performance. If you attempt to reduce the speed of your fans manually and don't really know what you're doing, there's every likelihood that your computer will overheat, crash, and (literally) burn.

What can I do about it?
● Drop back from maximum performance in the power plan
● Buy a cheap laptop stand
● Don't manually tinker with fan speeds!

WHEN I SWITCH ON MY COMPUTER, I SEE A DEMAND FOR MONEY TO GIVE ME MY FILES BACK. WHAT SHOULD I DO?

Malware has got nastier and nastier over the years, and these kinds of 'ransomware' attacks are horrible.

If you're lucky, it's just a chancer who's trying to get you to pay without doing any real damage to your computer; if you're not, they've encrypted your files and there may be no guaranteed way of getting them back.

There are many different types of ransomware and it's impossible to give advice that can cover all eventualities. If you've been the victim of a ransomware attack and you feel you're in over your head when applying some of the remedies below, then seek professional help. You can do greater damage if you get it wrong.

Our primary piece of advice would be don't pay the ransom. Yes, there are certainly many cases where paying a ransom has returned the victim's files, but there's no guarantee it will. They could take your money and run. Worse, you don't know what the attackers have left behind on your computer. Will they repeat the trick in six months' time, knowing they've got someone here who's willing to pay? Don't give into the temptation.

The first thing to ascertain is how bad the attack is. If you can get past or close the ransom screen and open the files on your computer, that's normally a good sign. That's usually an indication that the attacker was bluffing and hasn't encrypted your files. It may just be a pop-up that's appeared from a website or it may be something deeper – try performing a full scan of your system with your antivirus software to see if it detects anything nasty installed.

If you can't get past the screen or cannot open files on your computer (such as photos and documents), then it's likely to be one of the nastier variants.

At this point, the next thing to do is to disconnect your computer from the internet/home Wi-Fi so that you don't infect any other machines on the same network. If there's a ransom note or warning message on the screen, use your smartphone to take a photo of it for future reference.

If you have a full, up-to-date backup of your infected PC, our strong advice would be to wipe your PC clean by reinstalling Windows from scratch. (See the question on how do I reinstall Windows on page 100). That way you can be sure nothing nasty is left on your system. Just make sure you check the backup on another system first and ensure the ransomware hasn't infiltrated the backup too.

If your files have been encrypted, but you can get past the warning screen, then you can try downloading a decryptor that reverses the encryption of your files. Visit **nomoreransom.org** on your smartphone or another uninfected device, then enter any website address or bitcoin address the ransomware is asking you to send money to in the box provided. If the ransomware demand matches one on the site's database, you may be able to download a decryptor that puts all your files back to normal. Even if the decryptor works, run your antivirus software to make sure all traces of the ransomware are removed. We'd even be tempted to wipe clean and start again once we had a full backup, just to be sure.

Some ransomware encrypts files and then deletes the original copies. If you can't find a decryptor and have used antivirus software to remove the malware from your system, try running software such as Shadow Explorer (**shadowexplorer.com**), which can recover deleted files.

If none of that works and you don't have an adequate backup, seek professional help before throwing in the towel and wiping the computer.

What can I do about it?
- Check whether you can still open files
- Restore your PC from a backup
- See if you can download a decryptor or revive deleted files

WHY AM I GETTING A 'THIS APP NEEDS TO BE UPDATED' ERROR ON MY MAC?

Buckle up, folks. This one's going to get a wee bit geeky, about as geeky as we get in this book, because it's necessary to know the background to understand why you're getting this error message.

Around 2005, Apple (and other computer manufacturers) started the shift towards 64-bit hardware. 64-bit processors are hugely more powerful than the 32-bit processors that went before them, and allow the computer to use greater quantities of memory (RAM), among other benefits.

To take maximum advantage of the 64-bit hardware, both the operating system and the applications for it ideally need to be written in 64-bit code. But because there were still so many 32-bit systems out there, we've been gradually shifting from 32-bit to 64-bit software over the past 15 years. 64-bit machines can run old 32-bit software, but it's not as efficient as running 64-bit code.

Apple first shipped a 64-bit version of macOS back in 2009 and has been releasing 64-bit versions of its software ever since. The vast, vast majority of software written today is 64-bit, but there is some old 32-bit software out there that people still use that hasn't been updated.

With the release of macOS Catalina (10.15) in October 2019, Apple finally reached a tipping point. It said it would no longer support those old 32-bit apps, making macOS 64-bit only. Consequently, if you attempt to run old 32-bit software on Catalina, you'll see an error message telling you your 'app needs to be updated'. The program simply won't run.

If you're lucky, the software developer of the original app will have since released a 64-bit version of the software, but that will often mean you need to pay for the upgraded version.

If there's no new version, the only alternative is to stay on an older version of macOS, but that (a) may not be possible if you've already upgraded your system, and (b) comes with other disadvantages, such as a lack of new features and, eventually, security updates.

Unless that old 32-bit is absolutely business-critical or does a job no other piece of software can do, it's probably time to bite the bullet and upgrade the app, or find an alternative that does a similar job.

To find out if you've got any 32-bit apps on your Mac, click on the Apple menu in the top-left corner, select About This Mac and then click System Report. Select Legacy Software in the sidebar. Any software listed here is 32-bit. If that's blank, click Applications in the sidebar and scan the list of apps that appears. If 'no' appears in the column labelled '64-Bit (Intel)', that too is a 32-bit app.

What can I do about it?

- Look for an updated version of the app from the same developer
- Stick on macOS X 10.14 or older

MY COMPUTER KEEPS CRASHING – HOW DO I START IN SAFE MODE?

If your computer's about as stable as a lilo in rough seas, you're probably looking for the lifeboat of Windows Safe Mode. But it's not as easy to find as it once was. Let us be your lighthouse (we'll never use this metaphor again, promise).

Safe Mode, for those unfamiliar with its work, is a mode that strips down the operating system to its bare basics, limiting access to connected devices, installed software and even the internet. The idea is that if you've run into a problem that keeps causing your computer to fall over, you boot into Safe Mode to see if it's an inherent problem with the computer itself or something you've recently plugged in or installed. If the computer is stable in Safe Mode, you can start trying to diagnose the problem by, for example, disconnecting recently added devices, uninstalling software, or reversing updates to Windows or drivers.

In Windows 10, there are two versions of Safe Mode: bog-standard Safe Mode and Safe Mode With Networking, which leaves the internet connection intact. That can be handy if you need to download updated drivers for a device, for example.

You get to both via the same method. If you're able to keep Windows running for at least a minute or two, go to Settings, select Update & Security, and click the Recovery option. Under Advanced Startup, select Restart Now (obviously make sure you've saved any unsaved work first!).

When your PC restarts, you should see a blue screen with three options on it – choose Troubleshoot, then Advanced Options, Startup Settings, and Restart once more.

Once your PC restarts for the second time, you'll be given a list of options. Press the **4** key on your keyboard to boot into Safe Mode or press **5** for Safe Mode with Networking.

If your PC can't stand up in Windows long enough to fiddle with the Settings menu, go to this Microsoft support page for instructions on how to boot into Safe Mode from the sign-in screen or if you can't get anything but a black or blank screen: **bit.ly/34QnPQA**.

Once you're in Safe Mode, don't be alarmed if your graphics look all blurry, or external monitors or devices don't work. That's what's meant to happen. Once you've finished in Safe Mode, simply restart the PC as normal and it should go back to full-blown Windows so you can see if you've managed to fix your problem.

Macs also have a Safe Mode – called Safe Boot just to be typically different. To access this, all you need do is hold down the **SHIFT** key while the computer boots up. You can let go of the **SHIFT** key once you see the Apple logo and a progress bar appear on screen. Once again, a reboot will put the Mac back to normal.

What can I do about it?

- Access Safe Mode via the Windows 10 Settings menu (steps outlined above)
- Hold down **SHIFT** while the computer boots to put a Mac in Safe Boot

WINDOWS WON'T OPEN A FILE BECAUSE IT 'HASN'T GOT AN APP ASSOCIATED WITH IT'. WHAT DO I DO?

You've downloaded a file from a website, clicked on it and absolutely naff all has happened, except an annoying little pop-up message has appeared. 'The file does not have an app associated with it for performing this action. Please install an app or, if one is already installed, create an association in the Default Apps Settings page'.

It's one of those error messages that is about as much help as a dead wasp floating in your wine glass. 'Please install an app'? Which one? The first thing you need to do is work out what type of file you're trying to open. Right-click on the file and select Properties. In the window that appears, you should see Type of file listed, along with a three- or four-letter filename type (such as .odt or .indd).

Now, the easiest thing to do is Google that file type. In the examples above, for instance, you'd soon find out that .odt is a text document that can be opened by free word processing packages such as LibreOffice, while .indd is an Adobe InDesign file that must be opened with that particular piece of software.

If a quick Google search doesn't help, the excellent **fileinfo.com** should help identify what the file is.

This message can also appear after you've updated a piece of software to a new version, and all its file associations have been lost.

Consequently, when you go to open a certain file type – a spreadsheet, say, or a certain type of image file created in Photoshop – Windows can't remember what software to open it with.

To overcome this problem, you basically need to reintroduce Windows to the software in question. Normally, the easiest way to do this is to right-click on the file and choose Open With. A window will appear that allows you to select which app to open the file with. If the app you want isn't listed, select Look For Another App On This PC and then navigate to the app in question from the Programs folder that will open.

If that doesn't work, type 'default' into the Windows search bar and open the Default Apps setting. Now, click on Choose Default Application By File Type. Down the left of the screen you'll find a huge long list of file types. Find the one you want, then click Choose a Default next to it. Select the software you want to use for that particular type of file.

What can I do about it?
- Select file properties to identify the file type
- Right-click on file and choose Open With to find the relevant app
- Or use the Windows Default App settings

WHY HAS THE WINDOWS 10 SEARCH BOX GONE MISSING?

There's a delicious irony to your computer's search bar going AWOL. After all, where on earth do you go looking for it?

Luckily, this is one of those problems that is (normally) very easy to actually solve. Helpfully, it also gives us an opportunity to talk about rearranging that search bar and making more use of the limited space on the taskbar.

Firstly, to restore the search bar back to its rightful place on your screen next to the Start button, right-click on any blank space on the taskbar (the bar that normally sits at the bottom of the screen in Windows). Next you need to click on Search, and you'll probably see a tick next to Hidden. Click on Show Search Box and all should be well again.

While you were in that screen, you probably noticed another option there that you might not have come across before. The halfway house is to Show Search Icon. What this does it put a small, magnifying glass icon on your Windows taskbar, which takes up only a fraction of the valuable real estate at the bottom of the screen. If you often find you're running out of space on the taskbar because you've got too many programs pinned to it, this is a way of saving space without sacrificing app shortcuts.

Note that you don't have to have the search bar or icon visible at all to access Windows search. If you press the ⊞ **Windows** key + **S** simultaneously, the search facility will open.

What can I do about it?

- Access the search options by right-clicking on the taskbar
- Choose whether you want the full bar back or just a search icon

HOW DO I GET RID OF THE AWFUL CORTANA?

Cortana rivals Clippy, the animated paperclip, as the Microsoft 'assistant' people would cheerfully throttle with their bare hands. Microsoft's Alexa rival is built into Windows, and the only time most people come across it is when they accidentally say something vaguely like 'Hey, Cortana' and it fires up by accident.

If you've had enough of being interrupted by an unwanted voice assistant, or even want to replace Cortana with the much more useful Alexa, here's how to do it. First, some good news. Microsoft has now decided to 'de-emphasise' Cortana, making her more of an app than a built-in part of Windows. So, in Windows 10 version 2004 onwards, you have to actively sign into the Cortana app before the voice commands kick in.

If you're still running an older version of Windows 10 and want to stop Cortana chirping up, type 'Cortana' into the Windows 10 search bar and click on Cortana Permissions. Now click on Talk To Cortana on the left-hand side of the window. Turn off the 'Hey Cortana' invocation, the keyboard shortcut, and the Lock Screen option. If you're running your laptop on battery power, this will actually save a slice of battery life, as the microphone won't be permanently turned on, listening for your holler.

Now, back on the Windows desktop, you've probably noticed the circular Cortana orb next to the search bar. If you're not using Cortana, that's a waste of valuable space, so right-click on any empty space on the taskbar and untick the option that says Show Cortana Button. That should be the last you hear from Microsoft's Interrupter-In-Chief.

If you've got Amazon speakers all over your home and you're well used to conversing with Alexa, you might choose to replace Cortana with Alexa instead. To do that, go to the Windows Store and download the free Alexa app.

When you first fire up the app, you'll be given the option to turn on hands-free mode, which means you can say 'Alexa' to your computer (provided it has a mic, of course) and treat it like one of Amazon's speakers. The Alexa app for Windows doesn't quite have the full range of features that you get with a dedicated Amazon Echo speaker. You can't play music from third--party apps such as Spotify, for example, nor make free telephone calls. But most of the features are switched on and Alexa is a damned sight more useful than Microsoft's computerised PA.

What can I do about it?

- Disable Cortana from the Cortana Permissions setting
- Remove the Cortana button from the Windows taskbar
- Install the free Alexa app if you want a worthwhile replacement

I DON'T THINK MY PC HAS UPDATED TO THE LATEST VERSION OF WINDOWS – HOW DO I FORCE IT TO DO SO?

In the good old days, you knew roughly where you stood with Windows. You had Windows XP or Windows 7 or, although you'd never admit it publicly, Windows Vista. There was a clear distinction between the different versions and confusion was minimal.

Nowadays, things are a bit more complicated. Windows 10 has been out for five years at the time of writing, but the Windows 10 that first shipped in 2015 is a very different beast to the latest version that's available today.

Twice a year, Windows 10 gets what's known as a feature update, where new bells and whistles are added to the operating system. Nominally these are meant to happen in March and September, and so the March 2019 update was known as version 1903 (third month in 2019), while the autumn update was called version 1909. So how do you know if you've got the latest update and what can you do about it if you haven't?

To find out what version you're currently running, type 'about' into the Windows 10 search box and then click on the About Your PC option. Scroll down the page that appears and under the Windows Specifications heading, you should see which version you're on.

Now, don't be too perturbed if it's October and you're still stuck on the March update. These releases often slip – version 1909 didn't get released to the public until mid-November, for example. To check out which is the latest release, visit **docs.microsoft.com/en-us/windows/release-information** and look at the release dates.

If your PC is running an old version but a new one has only been released in the past couple of weeks, don't sweat too much. Microsoft staggers these releases so that the whole world isn't trying to download a massive update at the same time. It also means the whole planet doesn't have broken PCs if the early upgraders discover nasty bugs (this happens more often than Microsoft would like to admit).

However, if you're months or even years out of date on a new release, it's time to investigate. First thing to do is type 'update' into the search bar and click Check For Updates. This screen should reveal if you've got any updates pending. Sometimes you need to install minor updates before the big twice-annual updates will appear, so fetch yourself a cup of tea and prepare for a few system restarts.

Windows will, by default, automatically download and install updates these days, but it is possible to pause or defer updates. The Update screen should reveal if you've turned either of those on by mistake, and you can either click to unpause an update, or click the Advanced Options link and set the number of days to defer a feature update to zero.

It is possible that an update won't be offered to your machine, either because it's getting on a bit and doesn't meet the minimum requirements, or because Microsoft has scanned your system and found something that may conflict with the latest version. In these instances, there's nothing you can do to force the update. If it's a conflict bug, then the problem may be resolved in time (when your PC manufacturer issues a driver update, for example). If your PC doesn't meet the minimum requirements, then you're never going to get a feature update again and it's time to consider upgrading your computer.

What can I do about it?

● Check the About Your PC screen to find out what version you're on
● Check Microsoft's site to find out what the latest release is
● Use the Check for Updates screen to download any new updates

MY USB HARD DISK IS NOT RECOGNISED WHEN I PLUG IT INTO MY COMPUTER?

We've all done the USB hokey-cokey: put the square plug in, the square plug out, in, out, in, out, shake it all about... and still Windows won't recognise the hard disk! So how do you make Windows acknowledge the disk you're shoving into its ports?

There are a few things to try. First, open the Windows Device Manager – by searching for that phrase in the Windows 10 search box – and see if you can find the hard disk. It might be listed under Disk Drives. If you can see the drive in question, right-click on its listing and click Uninstall.

Now unplug the disk drive from the machine, reboot the PC, plug it back in and the hard disk's software driver should load automatically, hopefully allowing you to see the drive's contents in Windows Explorer.

If that fails, it's time to move up the chain a little. Go back into the Device Manager, click on Universal Serial Bus controllers, and then right-click to uninstall all the devices listed here. Note that if you have a USB mouse, you will likely lose temporary access to this. When you've uninstalled everything, reboot the PC and the drivers should (if you're connected to the internet) reload themselves. Plug your hard disk back in and hopefully now it will get the recognition it deserves.

No? Then it's time to take a fresh tack. Right-click on the Windows 10 Start button and select Disk Management. If you can see your disk listed in the drives at the top of the screen, right-click on it and select Change Drive Letter And Paths. Now click the Change button and give it a letter in the middle of the alphabet, such as M, that no other drive is likely to use. For some reason, simply assigning a drive a letter sometimes makes it visible in Windows. Ours is not to reason why...

If you're still seeing no signs of life and you're using a laptop on battery power, then let's just check the computer isn't quietly putting your USB ports to sleep. Search for 'power plan', open the Edit Power Plan setting, and select the Change Advanced Power Settings link. Under USB settings, change the USB Selective Suspend Setting to Disabled for both battery and when plugged in, and see if that makes a difference when you plug in your disk drives.

If all of that still draws a blank, it may be that there's a fault with the drive itself. Try plugging it into another computer to see if it's just sulking with your machine or if it's completely given up.

What can I do about it?
- Reinstall the disk drive
- Reinstall the USB controller drivers
- Assign the drive a letter in Windows

I KEEP GETTING STRANGE POP-UPS IN MY BROWSER... AND THERE'S A NEW SEARCH BAR AT THE TOP OF THE SCREEN. WHAT'S GOING ON?

This sounds like a nasty case of downloaditis. More specifically, you've inadvertently downloaded some horrific piece of adware that is blasting you with pop-ups and trying to redirect all your searches to an appalling Google clone, making your computing life a misery.

The first step is to try to disinfect your browser and disable any browser add-ons or extensions that this irritating adware has brought with it. In Chrome, for instance, type **chrome://extensions** into the address bar and remove any extensions that you don't want or recognise. Other browsers have different means of managing add-ons/extensions, but they're generally all available from the browser's main Settings menu.

Handily, Chrome also has a mini virus-checker of its own that can find and remove dodgy software from your browser and your computer. Click on the Chrome menu button (the three dots at the top of the screen) and then click Settings. Scroll down to the bottom of the screen and select Advanced Settings. Then click Clean Up Computer, and Chrome will scan your system for any nasties. Whilst you're there, go back one screen and select Restore Settings To Their Original Defaults to put Google back as the search engine.

The next step is to find out if there's any lingering adware that's installed itself in Windows. This often runs in the background, attempting to reinfect your browser if you delete nuisance extensions or toolbars, so it's best to chop it off at the knees. Use the Windows search facility to find the Add or Remove Programs setting in Windows and then scour that list for anything unfamiliar or iffy-sounding.

This can be tricky, because these malware programs often disguise themselves as something genuine-sounding, such as Pic Enhance or CheckMeUp. Look at the 'installed on' date next to the program's listing. If you're sure you've not installed anything in the past fortnight and there's a new program there from a week ago, when you started seeing these problems, that's likely the culprit to remove. There may well be more than one of these programs.

Now it's time to let security software make sure that every trace of malware has been removed from your system. If you're using the built-in Windows antivirus, search for 'Defender', and then in the Windows Defender settings, choose Scan Options. Select the Windows Defender Offline scan and press Scan Now. Leave your system to do its thing – this may take half an hour and the computer will restart. Hopefully this will clear any remnants.

If using paid-for security software, run a full scan on your system.

What can I do about it?
- Remove any strange browser extensions
- Run Chrome's Clean Up Computer facility
- Remove any strange software using Add or Remove Programs

HOW DO I STOP MY COMPUTER GOING TO SLEEP WHEN I LEAVE THE ROOM FOR TEN MINUTES?

Computers are like security guards – leave them be for ten minutes and they'll nod off in the corner.

Your computer putting itself to sleep when not in use is normally a good thing. It turns off the screen and other power-munching components, consuming less electricity, although it will still keep ticking away in the background if you're doing something such as a virus scan or downloading a massive file.

Still, if you want to stop your computer nodding off quite so quickly – or even prevent it from going to sleep at all – then it's easily adjusted.

In Windows 10, type 'sleep' into the search bar and open the Power & Sleep settings. Here you'll see four options determining how long Windows waits to turn off the screen and how long before it puts the computer to sleep, with options for when running on battery power and when plugged in. Adjust these to whichever timeframe suits you, right up to never!

If you're running a Mac, click the Apple logo in the top-left corner and select System Preferences, then click on the Energy Saver setting. Here you'll find options for when to switch off the display, put hard disks to sleep, or to put the whole computer into what Apple wittily describes as a Power Nap.

What can I do about it?

- Adjust the Power & Sleep options in Windows 10
- Fiddle with the Energy Saver settings on a Mac

MY WINDOWS 7 PC KEEPS FLASHING UP WARNINGS THAT SUPPORT HAS ENDED. WHAT DOES THAT MEAN?

Windows 7 is probably the best and most popular version of Windows Microsoft has ever released. Which is why – almost a decade after it was replaced with the execrable Windows 8 – it still remains on millions of computers in active use today.

But Windows 7 has now reached the end of the road. Microsoft stopped officially supporting the operating system in January 2020, which means it won't receive fixes for critical security bugs. To make sure you're not blind to that danger, Microsoft flashes up annoying full-screen warnings every now and then, trying to convince you to upgrade to Windows 10.

It's unlikely Microsoft is going to relent with such badgering. In fact, it's only going to get worse. So, you're faced with two choices: carry on regardless and try to find ways to best protect your now vulnerable machine, or bow to Microsoft's wishes and upgrade.

Let's deal with the first option: bludgeoning on. Even if Microsoft is pulling up the drawbridge, it's likely that other companies will continue to supply antivirus software for Windows 7. At the time of writing, these included well-known brands such as Avast (**avast.com/windows-7-antivirus**) and Avira (**avira.com/en/free-windows-7-antivirus**).

To be clear, even the third-party security software can't mitigate against flaws in the operating system itself, so you are more vulnerable to attack. But if you have a working Windows 7 PC and can't face the cost or hassle of an upgrade, then at least make sure you've got some security software watching your back.

The other option is to upgrade. At the time of writing, there were still ways to upgrade from Windows 7 to Windows 10 for free. A quick Google should reveal how, but just make sure you're downloading Windows 10 from official Microsoft sources, not dodgy third-party sites.

Whilst Windows 10's system requirements aren't that much greater than Windows 7's, it's still questionable whether you should upgrade in place. Any Windows 7 system is going to be at least five years old, likely older. That means it's entering the phase where hard disks start to fail, power supplies go pop, and so forth. Unless you pop in more memory and replace the hard disk with an SSD, the experience is likely to be sticky – and if you're performing those upgrades, you're getting to the point where it would be more economical to replace the entire PC.

Another option is to install an alternative, more lightweight operating system on your Windows 7 PC and avoid the nagging and security fears altogether. Neverware's CloudReady (**neverware.com**) will effectively turn your old PC into a Chromebook, which is fine for basic browsing, email, and day-to-day tasks. Alternatively, you could install one of the more lightweight versions of Linux, such as Puppy Linux (**puppylinux.com**) to replace Windows. Again, if you mainly use your PC for browsing the web and reading your Gmail, you won't find too much difference between using Windows and Linux, and the new operating system should be faster.

What can I do about it?

- Seek out Windows 7 security software
- Upgrade to Windows 10
- Replace Windows 7 with CloudReady or a Linux operating system

THIS BOOK HASN'T ANSWERED MY COMPUTER PROBLEM. WHERE BEST TO TURN FOR ADVICE NOW?

Firstly, we're sorry your question wasn't answered – we did warn you at the start that we didn't have a prayer of answering them all. But even if we can't answer your specific question, there's probably someone who can, as long as you know how to look for the answers. Here, then, is our guide to solving the computer problems we didn't answer.

LOOK FOR SPECIFIC ERROR MESSAGES

Error code X45DYH003 might not mean much to you, but you can bet your pension that Google will have heard of it. Error messages can sometimes flash up on screen and disappear seconds later, so either try to take a photo of any error message code using your smartphone or quickly jot them down for future reference.

If you punch the precise error code into Google, you will nine times out of ten find that hundreds of others have had the same problem and find a solution. The problem is, everyone has their own solutions, so how do you know which one to trust?

BEWARE OF THE ARMCHAIR EXPERTS

The sites we would trust are ranked in the following order:

1. Manufacturer's own support site – if Google turns up an answer to your error code on the manufacturer's own site, you can be pretty sure it's going to work. Be warned that many manufacturers have user forums, where it's sometimes hard to distinguish between advice from the company's own experts and that of customers. Obviously, be wary that the latter may not have the first clue what they're talking about.

2. Technology websites – tech websites (such as, ahem, **bigtechquestion.com**) like answering people's questions, because it's a good way to get traffic to their websites from Google. Most of the time, they're paying people who know what they're talking about, too. Just be a little more circumspect about following advice from sites where anyone can submit answers (such as **wikihow.com**), as the quality of the advice varies enormously.

3. Reddit – you may have heard of Reddit for its more unsavoury forums, but it's also got a huge community of highly tech literate users. Reddit is broken down into what's known as subreddits – or individual topics – many of which are based on specific tech products. There's a MacBook subreddit (**reddit.com/r/macbook**), for example, one for Windows 10 (**reddit.com/r/Windows10**), and one for almost any computer manufacturer or piece of major software you can think of. The great thing about Reddit is that readers can 'upvote' posts, so if someone's given good advice, they're likely to have a high number of votes (the number next to the up/down arrows beneath their post).

4. User forums – forums are a mixed bag. They can be brilliant, especially when you're dealing with niche products with unusual problems or error messages. But they can also be populated by well-meaning but knowledge-light keyboard warriors offering duff advice. Be particularly wary of any advice telling you to apply highly technical fixes, such as editing a PC's registry. It's very easy to make a problem worse if you're outside of your comfort zone.

ONLINE MANUALS

Thick printed manuals are something from a bygone era, but many products still produce PDF manuals that you can either download from the manufacturer's website or find elsewhere online. Google the specific product name and 'manual' and see if anything comes up, but don't pay for them! Sites such as **manualsonline.com** are worth checking if Google lets you down – although it has 'see prices' next to its manuals, these are just adverts for products and you can view the PDFs for free. Google Books also allows you to thumb through a huge range of titles, such as the excellent For Dummies series, which might solve your computing problems.

PROFESSIONAL HELP

Sometimes we all need a bit of professional help. And though the thought of paying someone to repair your computer might grate, it's often more economical than buying a new one. The computer repair business isn't as healthy as it once was, because many laptop manufacturers have made their products much harder for even the professionals to repair. Still, do your best to find a reputable repairer – and by that, we don't necessarily mean the big chains. Check a company's Google reviews, sites such as **Checkatrade.com**, and even the Which Trusted Trader scheme (which doesn't have many computer repairers on its books, but you might get lucky and find one near you).

Also from Raspberry Pi Press

CODE THE CLASSICS
Volume 1

A 224-page hardback book that tells the stories of seminal videogames from the 1970s and 1980s – and then shows you how to create your own.

In this first volume, we show you how to remake five classic video games – ranging from Pong to Sensible Soccer, each representing a different genre. We interview the games' original creators and learn from their example, as well as utilise the art and audio engineering skills of two of the 1980s' most prolific games developers for our recreated versions of the games.